THERE WILL I SING

A BIOGRAPHY OF
RICHARD LEWIS CBE

For Sir George Christie,
with my very best wishes,
Noel Ross-Russell
July '96

THERE
WILL I SING

The making of a tenor

A BIOGRAPHY OF
RICHARD LEWIS CBE

Noel Ross-Russell

OPEN GATE PRESS
London

First published in 1996 by Open Gate Press
51 Achilles Road, London NW6 1DZ

British Library Cataloguing-in-Publication Programme
A catalogue record for this book is available from the British
Library.

ISBN 1 871871 29 8

Printed in Great Britain by
Hartnolls Ltd, Bodmin, Cornwall

To Elizabeth, who shared her life with Richard, and without whom this book could never have been written, and to Brenda, in love and friendship.

Contents

Acknowledgements   i
List of Illustrations   v
Foreword by Andrew Davis CBE   vii

Overture   1
Manchester 1914-1930   3
First Choices   8
The Chance to Sing   21
Conflict 1939-1945   33
New Beginnings   44
A Family Man   50
Voyage Round the World   71
Elizabeth   79
Moses and Aaron   97
Homeward Bound   104
Still Dreaming   112
Act 3   120
Curtain Up   127
Index   131
Discography   139

Acknowledgements

To Elizabeth Muir-Lewis and Brenda Webb, to whom this book is dedicated and whose support in so many ways made it possible.

To Mary Kellock, for her memories of life with Richard, and to the following for their contributions in interview and, where necessary, in letters: Lady Barbirolli, Dame Joan Sutherland, Eric and Gwyneth Mitchell, Mary Kirkby, Beryl Colclough, Richard Baker, Lady Rothnie, Herbert Barrett, Jack Brymer, Leo Kramer, Marjorie Thomas, Kay Chandler, Norman and Joan Carr, Janet Canetty-Clarke, John Carol Case, Martin Isepp, James Paul, Michael Kennedy, Phillip Langridge, Anthony Rolfe Johnson, Su Shanson, Norman Nelson, Luciano Pavarotti, Simon Streatfeild, Michael Preston-Roberts, Sir Georg Solti, Richard Valéry, Sir John Tooley, Christopher Yates, Adèle Leigh, Sir George Christie, Edward Morgan, Felix Aprahamian, Henrike Tempelaars, Michael and Huilee Lewis, Nigel Lewis, Grace Robertson, Godfrey Thurston Hopkins, Ian Partridge, Irene Bishop, Richard Bradburn and Anthony Hodges.

My grateful thanks to Andrew Davis for his touching *Foreword*, and to Joy Smith, who supported Richard with her presence in the audience on so many occasions and suggested the title of this biography: a line from Cardinal Newman's poem *The Dream of Gerontius*.

To my editor, Jeannie Cohen, for her wise counsel and endless patience.

Special thanks to my dear Adriana, who lived the book both day and night, and to our friends, Lee Bailey and Sarah Kurslake, who each gave me a key to their homes and respite from my telephone.

To Nicola Adams, who painstakingly typed my manuscript, and finally, to Georgie, who kept me company for hours and growled in all the right places.

My appreciation to the BBC, Glyndebourne Opera, Royal Opera House Covent Garden, Royal Academy of Music, Royal College of Music, Royal Northern College of Music, and to Eastbourne and Manchester Central Libraries for their helpful cooperation.

Noel Ross-Russell

Permissions

I am grateful for permission to use extracts from newspapers as follows:

Arbeiderbladet, Oslo – pages 41-42; The Times (© Times Newspapers Limited 1947, 26/8/53, 25/6/54, 19/5/62) – pages 60, 62, 67, 90; The Oxford Mail – page 60; The Birmingham Post – page 60; The Birmingham Mail – page 60; The Liverpool Evening Express – page 61; The Scotsman – page 61; The Telegraph – pages 62-3 (© The Telegraph plc, London, 1953); The Scottish Daily Express (© Express Newspapers Ltd) – page 62; The Daily Mail – page 62; The Liverpool Daily Post – page 67; The Manchester Guardian (© The Guardian, by kind permission) – page 68; The Financial Times – page 98; The Liverpool Post – page 99; The Washington Post – page 107; The Liverpool Post – page 114; The London Evening News – page 97

Every effort was made to trace the copyright holders of the following extracts, but without success. We should be delighted to hear from them.

The News Chronicle – page 48; The Evening World – page 60; The Glasgow Bulletin – page 65; The Glasgow Herald – page 66; The Star (Washington) – page 107; The New York Herald Tribune – page 127

I am also grateful to the following for permission to use photographs:

The Theatre Museum: cover picture of Richard Lewis as Aaron in *Moses and Aaron* (photograph by Houston Rogers, Theatre Museum, V&A). Mrs Guy Gravett: Guy Gravett photographs acknowledged *in situ*. The Yorkshire Post: photograph of Richard Lewis in Beverley Minster The Harvard Theatre Collection: photograph by Angus McBean of Richard Lewis as Peter Grimes Associated Press: photo of Richard Lewis receiving the CBE

Every effort was made to trace the following copyright holders, but without success. We should be delighted to hear from them.

David H. Fishman; Fotesa, Buenos Aires; François Martin, Geneva; Jack Woods, Warner Bros.

All photographs are acknowledged also *in situ* and in the list of illustrations.

I should like to thank Lady Barbirolli for allowing me to quote from Sir John Barbirolli's correspondence, and Luciano Pavarotti for allowing me to use his letter to Richard Lewis on the occasion of his 70th birthday.

List of Illustrations

Front cover:
Richard Lewis in *Moses and Aaron.*

Photographic plates:
Richard's mother.
Richard's father.
With Mary. Pilot and navigator, 1958.
Looking ahead with Michael. *Photo: The News, Adelaide*
A man of many parts.
With his much-loved Mercedes outside the RAH. *Photo: Downton's News Service*
With Michael. Commander of the British Empire. *Photo: Associated Press*
With Elizabeth at dinner.
Trees painted by Richard after his stroke.
St Andrew's University Doctor of Music.
At home in Wilmington. *Photo: Guy Gravett*
From the top, ladies and gentlemen.
Proud father with Nigel.
A good place to rest. Elizabeth found a spot for Richard's ashes years later.
Photo: Guy Gravett
Singing Britten with the Oslo Philharmonic.
Tom Thomas as Philippe in *The New Moon* December 1938.
Peter Grimes at Covent Garden.
Angus McBean photograph, Harvard Theatre Collection, The Houghton Library

Leopold Simoncau, friend and colleague.
With Joan Sutherland in *Don Giovanni* at Glyndebourne. *Photo: Guy Gravett*
As Captain Vere in *Billy Budd* with Stafford Dean and Harvey Alan.
Photo: David H. Fishman
With Frederica von Stade in *Ulysses* at Glyndebourne. *Photo: Guy Gravett*
With Geoffrey Parsons in Beverley Minster. *Photo: by courtesy of The Yorkshire Post*
Idomeneo at Glyndebourne with Luciano Pavarotti. *Photo: François Martin, Geneva*
Seeing the funny side of Otto Klemperer. *Photo: Illiffe, Allegro*
Chatting with Sir Michael Tippett. *Photo: Associated Press*
Taking in the sights of Buenos Aires with Sir Geraint Evans.
Photo: Fotesa, Buenos Aires
Presenting the Gold Medal of the ISM to Sir Alexander Gibson.
At Glyndebourne with Frederica von Stade.
With Mario Lanza in Hollywood. *Photo: Jack Woods, Warner Bros.*

Foreword

One of the first recordings I ever bought was of Elgar's *Dream of Gerontius*; for the better part of a year I could listen only to Part I and the opening of Part II while I saved my pennies for the second disk of the two-record set, but by the time I at last heard the climactic phrase 'Take me away', the artistry and sheer vocal magic of Richard Lewis had already become a vital part of life in my early teens.

Thus it was with a sense approaching awe that, almost twenty years later, I finally conducted this great work with him; it was a performance which I shall never forget, one which formed a bond of mutual respect and affection between us which made our subsequent infrequent, usually accidental, meetings a source of great delight.

In the intervening years I had heard him sing on many occasions in repertoire ranging from Elizabethan lute songs through Bach, Mozart and Mahler to the newest contemporary works (most memorable for me being his creation of the rôles of Mark and Achilles in the first two operas of another early and enduring idol, Michael Tippett). His versatility, to which his work at Glyndebourne alone would have been eloquent testimony enough, arose from his adventurousness, his extraordinary musical intelligence and above all, a deep poetic sense which made him one of the most moving artists of his time.

Noel Ross-Russell's book is enormously welcome for the light it sheds on a man who himself gloriously illuminated the lives of so many.

Andrew Davis CBE

Overture

The familiar, wholesome smell of the sweating animal as it struggled to maintain a hold on the slippery cobbles of Fairfield Street filled him with concern, for he loved the horse dearly and always did his best to limit its labour. He trailed the long whip gently over its flanks, merely as a reminder that they were together in the work, and concentrated on the road, watchful for any holes or loose stones which might prove troublesome. Thomas Thomas was that sort of man.

The overhead gas lamps were reflected in the polished surface, for it had been raining heavily throughout the night and a few scattered drops were still falling. He looked at the harness brasses which would need to be cleaned again at the end of the day, although it was certain to be raining the following morning. The area manager of the London Midland and Scottish expected a smart turnout come rain or shine, and Manchester saw more rain in a week than Llansantffraid in a month, or so it seemed to him.

He missed Wales desperately at times; still he had moved willingly when the job was offered, and Mary, Vera, and the baby appeared happy. He was thankful, for the money wasn't bad and outside the railway there was nothing at home other than work on the land and limited prospects. Money apart, his position was considered important because of the need to keep the railways running smoothly and he didn't envy the poor devils who were being called to serve in France.

They were approaching the station forecourt where the big man was to be picked up and he glanced at his watch anxiously. Good. Four minutes still to go. He braced his shoulders and tapped the top of his hat.

Manchester 1914-1930

This is the story of a man who dreamed and lived to see his dream fulfilled. Of a man who aspired to better things and believed his talent would provide the means. Of a man for whom the phrase 'good enough' had no meaning and who set out to build his castle brick by brick and, when the bricks were in short supply, waited patiently for God to lend a hand.

But we must start with the boy, born in Manchester on May 10th 1914, the second child of Thomas and Mary Thomas, and christened Thomas himself. (To distinguish father from son we will call the boy Tom, and indeed this was how he was known for the first thirty-two years of his life). His sister was older by eight years, and her name was Vera.

Thomas and Mary had come to Manchester from the small Welsh village of Llansantffraid, when Thomas was offered the job of coachman to the area manager of the L.M.S. Railway[*], and they set up home in the district of Ardwick, at 69 Baden Street. As for so many from Wales, two things counted more than anything else in their lives. The first was the Methodist Church, and the second was music. It seems that they were all musical to some extent, and Mary made sure that each one played their part. She herself played the harmonium and sang quite well. The hymns of the little chapel in Llansantffraid were among her earliest memories, and Vera and Tom were introduced to them as babies. Vera recalled her mother

_____

[*] London Midland and Scottish Railway Company

3

taking Tom on her lap and playing with one hand as she sang. Standing beside her the little girl joined in and turned the pages.

Outside the Bible, the Methodist Hymn Book was the most important book in the house and thanks to it, four part harmony became as natural as the ABC. In due course both children played the piano and experimented with a violin and clarinet which were kept in the cupboard under the stairs.

One of the reasons Thomas had accepted the job was the possibility of a better education for his children; and first of all Nansen Street Elementary, and later, Didsbury Central Secondary School, provided this.

By the time Tom was ten the family began to notice something about his singing that set him apart from the other children they knew, and they spoke confidentially (for they did not wish to presume) to someone well known in Methodist music circles, and already Vera's piano teacher. Another Tom: Tom Evans. Organist, choirmaster, and conductor of the Apollo Singers, he confirmed what the Thomases had thought might be the case. Tom Thomas was a boy with an unusually good soprano voice.

Due to his employment in an essential service, Thomas had been spared the trenches of the First World War and consequently his family had been less affected than some others. This did not mean there was money to throw about, far from it, but with careful economies, and Mary taking in washing and ironing, they could just manage piano lessons for Vera and singing lessons for Tom.

Ardwick was a mixed area in those days, combining respectable working-class homes with more prosperous dwellings, and quite a few professional men lived there. Thomas was proud of his position and his brushed suit and polished shoes reflected this. Mary was always neatly dressed and groomed and the children were never allowed to leave the house without a final checking of socks and hair. The values and attitudes planted in Llansantffraid were fostered in Ardwick, and no one was going to let the side down.

By 1924 Vera was a good pianist and while she remained at home Tom had his own accompanist at hand; a tremendous advantage for a singer. In Mr Evans, Tom was also fortunate, and though the day would come when the teacher's talents fell short of the pupil's needs and only the best would do, that day was still some way off.

In the meantime there were breathing exercises to work on and scales to be practised. Words to be learnt and melodies studied. Intonation, beauty of sound, phrasing, every element considered. Above all, the Welsh passion for language and its expression. The words must be understood by the singer and felt by the listener. No room for misunderstanding here, the message had to be unquestionable. The desire to communicate in this fashion was present in the boy to an unusual degree, and remained with him throughout his life.

Most singers come to accept their vocal talents as God-given, and as he grew older Tom became increasingly grateful for his gift and believed it was his duty to develop it fully. The fact that their voice is part of them sometimes leads singers to neglect the theory of music, something which no instrumentalist can possibly do. Organist and choirmaster that he was, Mr Evans insisted on Tom studying harmony and simple counterpoint from the beginning and was delighted when he took to these subjects like a duck to water. Is it possible that Tom's instincts were so accurate, that he could see ahead more than twenty years, and knew his career would require the most comprehensive musicianship? Between the age of ten and sixteen Tom took advantage of every opportunity to sing. At school, at home, when visiting friends, and certainly at church. No doubt he sang in the choir on occasion, but from the first he was recognised as a soloist and this was his greatest joy. There was no need to persuade Tom to sing; it was what he was born to do. It was also in his nature to enjoy competition and it was even more fun when he won.

His school reports were average, apart from English, Art and Music, and in these subjects he did well. At fourteen Tom was tall for his age and well developed physically, with only one obvious weakness; his eyes. He hated the glasses he was forced to wear and did without them whenever he could. He loved sports and never missed the chance to play football and cricket. The latter was his favourite and had music not been so strong in him, it is conceivable that he would have taken the game seriously. But music was strong in him, in fact each year it seemed to get stronger and there was no resisting it.

The county of Lancashire was noted for its music and the number of amateur festivals that took place. Manchester had its famous Hallé Orchestra and the best conservatory of music outside London. Perhaps one day Tom would study there, thought Mary, but who could be sure he would still be able to sing after his voice broke? That could be at any time of course, but he was big for his age.

His soprano voice was now at its best, and with Mr Evans' encouragement and Vera at the piano, Tom entered every festival he could. His record was remarkable and revealed not only an exceptional vocal talent, but a desire to excel. In the fourteen competitions Tom Thomas entered during this period he was placed first by the adjudicators thirteen times. On the day he failed, he came second. No boy soprano in Lancashire had so impressed the festival juries, but how much longer could it last? The answer came in his sixteenth year, which was also the year of his leaving Didsbury Central and starting work at the Calico Printers Association. Just a few more weeks and he would have recorded for the BBC in London.

We call it a broken voice and this suggests pain: however the pain, if there is any, is emotional rather than physical, and not every boy experiences the embarrassment which causes some not to speak more than is absolutely necessary during this stage in their development.

How this affected Tom we cannot be sure, but many boys possessed of good singing voices have spoken about their anguish when the first tell-tale signs of breaking occurred: the dismay caused by the fractured notes which substitute for the previously secure tones; the struggle to recapture the prized possession, until acceptance of the situation takes hold; and then, an equal determination not to sing again. If this sounds like our reaction to a love affair which has ended, then the comparison is valid, for it can be as painful. For Tom, it was a busy time, and leaving school and starting work must have occupied his mind. It also helped that Tom was not just someone with a voice, but a musician who could sing, and Mr Evans had seen boys through this a hundred times before. 'You must be patient. Give it time. Let it settle. Then we shall see what we have.'

First Choices

Patience was never easy to come by for Tom. The Thomases, especially Mary, were easily irritated and short-tempered when things didn't go according to plan, but Tom did have something else on which he could rely. It could be summed up in one word and he had been given a double helping. Determination. If he had to wait for his voice to return then he would, no matter how long it took. Two years, three years, four years. He sensed that the longer he waited, the better it might be, and in the meantime there was so much to learn.

He had heard people talk about the Royal Manchester College of Music[*] as being the place to study, that was if you had a professional career in mind. But did he have a professional career in mind? He didn't know. How could he? He had to wait and see what sort of voice emerged once the change from boy to man was over. It was a bit like waiting for a baby to arrive. No matter; he needed to be ready and he would be.

The Calico Printers Association, or CPA as it was generally known, became Tom's second home, although he would scarcely have described it as such. His school days at Didsbury Central had earned him his School Certificate, and his neat handwriting, polite behaviour and smart appearance made him ideal clerical material,

---

[*] Now called the Royal Northern College of Music following amalgamation with the Northern School of Music in 1973.

8

with the potential for management later on. In 1930 jobs were not growing on trees, and although the chaos in the labour market following the war had eased somewhat, without the right connections and a public, or grammar school education, a sixteen-year-old had few choices.

The office staff who became his colleagues were no better or worse than most other working-class youngsters, but to Tom they seemed uncouth. There was no swearing at home in Baden Street; Thomas and Mary saw to that. The coarse language of the office and the smutty stories swapped by the young men at the CPA came as a rude shock and he suffered the atmosphere with difficulty. He had not been taught to go along with the crowd; in fact the teachers of Didsbury Central who enforced good behaviour in the school regarded Tom as a model pupil. An example for others to follow. It set him apart and he had few close friends as a result. A more worldly-wise youth would have at least pretended to enjoy the rough humour, but Tom was not made for compromise and his disapproval must have been all too obvious. For the Thomases things were either right or wrong; there was no middle way. They lived their lives by the scriptures and this lifestyle isolated them from everyone other than the churchgoers they met each Sunday.

On the other hand Tom was a good-looking boy and the office girls were not slow to show their interest. The fact that he remained indifferent to their smiles served only to increase his attractiveness. Naturally he felt flattered by the attention he received, but the goal he had set himself was so securely placed, and the rules of church and home so much a part of him, that any temptation to stray was checked, and the girls turned their attentions to more likely candidates.

The long hours of boring clerical work were broken by a lunch break which Tom always spent away from the CPA. He loved to walk and the office was conveniently situated in the centre of Manchester close to the music shops and one or two pleasant milk bars. He could not afford to eat in restaurants, of course, and Mary packed his lunch each day, but an occasional milk shake in polished surroundings provided a blessed relief. If only the world could be shiny clean and free of dirt. It was all a question of choice, surely.

Good music, or cheap music? Good English, or vulgar speech? Good behaviour, or bad behaviour? Even things over which one had no control. Good weather, or bad weather? For Tom the choice was clear cut. People who chose badly puzzled him.

One might have expected the never-ending clerical work to quell any desire to write in his out of office hours, but the reverse was the case. If the CPA gave him anything, it gave him the under-standing that an organisation could not succeed without properly kept books: order books, receipt books, delivery books, account books; and since Tom was in the business of Tom Thomas – Tenor, or would be once the product arrived, he would start keeping his own.

To begin with these were inexpensive notebooks costing no more than a few pence: the kind he had used at school to record his homework assignments. This was reasonably satisfactory and allowed him to keep a check on things, but some of the notes required a date attached to them and this inevitably led to the idea of a diary. Once started, Tom was meticulous in keeping up to date, and because he had few friends, his diary became the repository of his hopes and wishes.

For his biographer this has been an invaluable source of information, since Tom kept a yearly diary and only a few are missing from 1934 onwards. Regrettably, the war years are absent: either because soldiers were discouraged from keeping diaries which might contain information valuable to the enemy; or because, due to the uncertainty of life and the fact that one was no longer a free agent, the purpose of diary keeping was lost.

The publishers of diaries generally provide a place for the owner's name and address and a few other pieces of information, and it is an example of Tom's consistency that every possible item is noted year after year. Date of birth, next of kin, insurance policy number, bank account numbers, car registration, camera number, these are just the obvious ones. Had the diary asked for shirt collar size, Tom would have filled it in!

And so those first years at the CPA passed and one or two good friends were found. His constant companion on the lunch time walks and for cinema visits was Ken Timms, and when Millie Charles joined the office she provided his first romantic attachment. Cricket continued to interest him and he played for the Association and scored a few runs, but a team game was not the same as an individual sport and tennis became an alternative relaxation when the weather was good. By the time he was eighteen his voice had settled down, or rather up, for his speaking voice was always on the high side, and he made plans to start lessons again as soon as the time was right. Six feet tall, he was splendidly built for swimming, and he went to the pool whenever he could. His reserved nature occasionally gave way to outbursts of high spirits, and when he took off his glasses Millie found him irresistible. Quite sophisticated: he even smoked!

Another year passed and his vocal efforts in the bathroom and on Sundays at church led him to believe he was ready to begin lessons again. He called to see Mr Evans and tried a few things in his recently acquired tenor voice. What do you think? he asked nervously. 'I think you know,' Evans replied. 'It's better than ever.' They arranged some dates for lessons and Tom hurried home to tell Mary and Thomas.

It is interesting to see the notes Tom made to reinforce his ambition. He was twenty.

1st December 1934

1. I must really get down to my music.

2. I must trust to God's guidance.

3. Read more – and cultivate my manner of speech.

4. I must not let the ridicule, the low level and standard of intelligence etc of the office have any influence upon my ideals and ambitions.

5. Must keep my head up and aim as best as I can for the highest and best.

28th December 1934

I am anxious. My ambitions and desires are very great, too great perhaps for the circumstances at home...I want to raise myself out of the state of ignorance I am now in. I want to understand, to be able to converse intelligently, to speak in a manner which is acceptable in anyone's company. I want to be of use in this world, to anybody, high or low. But music, I feel is to be the dominant thing in my life....

1st January 1935

The beginning of a new year. What has it in store for me? I don't know. All that I do know is that I must carry on, to work hard and trust to God's guidance.

2nd January 1935

My emotions are great, especially after last night. I went to see Richard Tauber in Blossom Time at the Theatre Royal. My emotions were that deep while I was watching the picture that I felt I could have cried. He sang so beautifully....I wondered if I could possibly get to such a level and standard of musical understanding, not only in singing but in theory, composition etc....I must struggle and help my parents in their sacrifice.... We are not poor, but the circumstances at home are just ordinary.... father has just a moderate waged occupation.... I am always hoping that some day I will be able to converse and speak intelligently and in a refined manner. You see, I feel that in my life I must aim at something high....

8th January 1935

My ambition to be a singer, to know the art of music. Music is my one desire. I want to be wrapped up in that and nothing else.

24th April 1935

Lately my heart has just simply been burning with the desire for the knowledge of music. Nobody knows the feelings I experience at times. It is a great aching desire.... I feel as though I am imprisoned, locked up inside a business house, where I am compelled to spend from 8.30-5.30 daily in its odour filled room.... Wouldn't it be wonderful if I could leave this place.... and spend my whole time studying the art to which I am deeply drawn.... I am young and full of ambition and there is always the future to look forward to. I must struggle on.

Books borrowed from the Library:

Lessons in Harmonising – C. Harris
Control of the Breath – Doddo & Lickley
The Singing Voice – Passé
The Voice – Stanley & Maxfield
Authentic Voice Production – Shaw
Singing – Witherspoon

Complete Opera Book – Kobbé
Story of Wagner's Ring

Quotations admired:
'Concentration and absorption are the only clues to success in music as in life' Arthur Schnabel
'Ignorance never settles a question' Disraeli
'Give light and the people will find their own way' Dante
'The infallible receipt for happiness is to be good' H. Drummond
'It is right to be contented with what we have, never with what we are' Sir James Mackintosh

Towards the end of 1935 Tom bemoaned the fact that committed church members though they were, his parents, and in particular his mother, viewed heaven and earth as two quite separate entities. Cut off from one another.

Perplexed. Is that the word? Oh, if only Mother had a deep realisation of God's love. His guidance and his help. His comfort and power, wouldn't that be great? It would help her in her worries and difficulties and domestic troubles. It could help her to broaden her mind so as to see other people's views and not be so stubborn. Oh, if only she (and Father also) had the same experience and views as myself, we could speak along the same lines and be of one understanding. If only they could understand my ideas.... My desires and ambitions are perhaps overwhelming me.... I must try to remember I am not yet 21.... I feel there is a great time ahead if I am spared and I believe that God will guide me that way.

1935 was the year of the Silver Jubilee and Tom felt almost as strongly about the King and Queen as he did about God. His diary for the year makes this very clear. *'The King and Queen have now reigned for twenty five years,'* he writes in the inside cover, and as if confirmation were needed a special issue halfpenny stamp is stuck there. His respect for the Royal Family verges on reverence. Every day of this celebratory year is carefully recorded, with special reference to the weather. Perhaps this accounts for the pleasure he reveals whenever the day is fine. Several days in a row lead him to express his gratitude quite passionately, but he is desperately unhappy at the CPA office. He calls it *'that terrible place.'* The gossip that passes for conversation bores him and the language used causes him to despair. Ken is a loyal friend, and they keep up their routine of walking together when the weather is good. Sometimes they call at the BBC. and pick up pamphlets of interest to Tom. These are intended to accompany broadcast talks and are welcomed by those eager to know more. In June of this year a programme by Sir Walford Davies, the composer famous for his *Elegiac Melody* and Master of the King's music was entitled 'Chords that Matter'. Tom's interest in the theory of music was quite profound. He set aside time at night to study harmony (Keighley's text book) and he played the piano with a view to accompanying himself in practise and to be an all round musician, not simply a singer. *'I must keep this up,'* he writes. *'One day this will be beneficial to me.'* His studies with Mr Evans continued, but he experienced some dissatisfaction with his lessons, a disappointment which grew as the voice developed. He admired Tauber and Borgioli and received advice from Borgioli after attending a recital. He called him *'my tenor'*. On 8th December Tom sang his first *Messiah* at Gransmore Road Methodist Church. It was successful and he enjoyed himself.

At the beginning of 1936 the musical film *Heart's Desire* starring Richard Tauber was showing in Manchester. Tom had waited a long time for the film to be released and was not disappointed. His analysis of Tauber's singing is interesting. For a fan – and there was no doubting his enthusiasm for the great Austrian tenor – his observations are precise and proportionate.

8th February 1936

Tauber isn't the greatest tenor of today, but he is very popular and has a charming voice. I like him because his attitude is so acceptable... He is an exponent of expression and his head notes are perfect. His lower notes are perhaps lacking good resonance but his higher range is powerful.... The position of his tongue, as I could see on several occasions, must come naturally to him.... It must be a great risk singing for the talkies, as some voices are unacceptable by the microphone. The technical apparatus is too sensitive, but Tauber's timbre seems to be very suitable. He is a great singer and I admire him very much.

Tom's eyesight was always weak and he was obliged to wear glasses which he found very inconvenient, particularly when singing. After a concert at the Central Hall in Oldham Street with his good friend, Fred Bradbury (a baritone with whom he would often share the programme in solos and duets) he complained to his diary about his spectacles getting in the way. *'I am very conscious of their presence on my face. I must try to do without them.'*

His lessons with Mr Evans may have been disappointing, but at least he was enlarging his repertoire. The Hazel Grove Festival was considered a challenge and he entered with Handel's 'He has his Mansion' and an aria with which he would be associated for the rest of his life – Coleridge-Taylor's 'Onaway Awake' from *Hiawatha*. On the day of the Festival he left the office to get his train at London Road Station with just ten minutes to spare and got to the hall by the skin of his teeth. He was successful in the preliminary round, but in the finals he forgot his music in the changing room and had to dash from the stage to get it. This meant a run up and down stairs and he returned to the platform out of breath. Somehow he recovered and sang very well. 'Never mind that mishap,' said the adjudicator who placed him second, 'You've a fine voice. A gift from God.' Second wasn't good enough for Tom, who believed the cup should have been his. He wouldn't forget his music again.

The tenor voice is not a common voice, baritone being the normal adult male pitch. However, Tom's voice was naturally high. After the spectacular success of his boyhood years, Tom's development as a tenor was by comparison rather slow. (But this was only to be expected.) A question mark hangs over every man blessed as a boy with a good treble voice. Notable at this time was Ernest Lough, whose recording of 'Hear My Prayer – Oh, for the Wings of a Dove' brought fame to the chorister of the Temple Church. Although Lough continued to record after his voice had broken, the adult voice was merely a pleasant baritone and no significant career followed. Tom's case was different. The pitch indicated that a 'genuine' tenor existed and throughout adolescence and young manhood the voice developed month by month and year by year. Mr Evans may have lacked many things Tom sought in a teacher, but he did realise that his pupil had a remarkable gift and that if nature and patience were allowed to take a hand, the result should be exceptional.

Tom was much involved with the children's choir at the Wesleyan Church to which the Thomas family belonged, and trained the children for choral competitions. This certainly helped him as a musician, as did his piano playing and harmony, and slowly the musician, as well as the singer emerged. Slowly too the man.

Lawn tennis, table tennis, cricket and swimming were all sports he enjoyed, and he brought to each the same professional approach he applied to his music. This desire to win however, was not always appreciated in the circles in which he mixed, and was fundamentally at odds with the spirit of the times, when participation was the thing, not winning.

By now his repertoire included the *Messiah* and he revelled in the demanding tenor solos. Performance anxiety was not a problem at this stage, or indeed at any stage in his life, and perhaps the amount of solo singing he had done as a boy was helpful. Undoubtedly a rock-like belief in self, supported by a profound religious conviction, was the basis for this.

Tom's interests naturally included the opposite sex and one or two girls caught his eye at work and at the tennis club. He was very romantic, to judge by his diary, but extremely reserved. He appreciated the countryside and made frequent reference to the trees, birds singing, the sky at night and similar. Of tremendous importance to Tom was the weather. He was almost obsessional in his longing for a sunny day.

His interest in what people wore was also unusual. Detailed descriptions of the clothes at several weddings take up considerable space in his diary. He even drew the dress of a bridesmaid and drew it well. Not the stuff of most twenty-two year old men, but the interest was an authentic one. As with everything else, Tom's wish to see the world beautifully dressed went hand-in-hand with

ichard's mother.

Richard's father.

'ith Mary. Pilot and navigator, 1958.

ooking ahead with Michael. *Photo: The News, Adelaide*

A man of many parts.

With his much-loved Mercedes outside the RAH.

With Michael. Commander of the British Empire.

With Elizabeth at dinner.

rees painted by Richard after his stroke. St Andrew's University Doctor of Music.

From the top, ladies and gentlemen.

At home in Wilmington. *Photo: Guy Gravett* Proud father with Nigel.

Singing Britten with the Oslo Philharmonic.

Photo: Guy Gravett

A good place to rest. Elizabeth found a spot for Richard's ashes years later.

Tom Thomas as Philippe in *The New Moon* December 1938.

Peter Grimes at Covent Garden. *Angus McBean photograph Harvard Theatre Collection, The Houghton Librar*

With Joan Sutherland in *Don Giovanni* at Glyndebourne.

opold Simoneau, friend and colleague.

Captain Vere in *Billy Budd* with Stafford Dean and Harvey Alan.

With Frederica von Stade in *Ulysses* at Glyndebourne.

Photo: Guy Gra

Photo: by courtesy of The Yorkshire Post

With Geoffrey Parsons in Beverley Minster.

Photo: François Martin, Ger

Idomeneo at Glyndebourne with Luciano Pavarotti

...eing the funny side of Otto Klemperer.

Photo: Illiffe, Allegro

Photo: Associated Press

...hatting with Sir Michael Tippett.

Photo: Fotesa, Buenos Aires

Taking in the sights of Buenos Aires with Sir Geraint Evans.

Presenting the Gold Medal of the ISM to Sir Alexander Gibson.

At Glyndebourne with Frederica von Stade.

With Mario Lanza in Hollywood.

Photo: Jack Woods, Warner Br

his appreciation of refined speech and manners. He may not have been born into the society to which he was naturally attracted, but his sensibilities were not to be compromised with. One suspects that this was closely linked to his religious view that if man behaved himself, the world could be the beautiful place God intended. Throughout his life Tom cherished a reverence for three things. The first was God and his son Jesus Christ. The second was music and Wolfgang Amadeus Mozart. The third was the Royal Family and Commonwealth.

In 1937 his church interests were at their greatest. A cousin, Leslie Jones, was invited to preach at the Welsh Chapel in Weaste, and Tom was critical: *'Leslie is a very good preacher but his delivery lacks fire, his articulation is overdone.'*

The office made its demands, with stocktaking occupying him in early January. Many evenings he finished at nine or ten o'clock which reduced the time available for serious music study, but at least this meant extra money which was used to buy sheet music at Wright Greaves' in the Royal Exchange, or books like the complete Grove's dictionary. He was re-elected to the committee of the tennis club and there were more amateur engagements at various churches in Manchester. He was now first choice for these programmes. St Stephen's, Stockport Road, invited him to sing but he had reservations about the organist. He was right to be concerned. On the night of the concert there were passages in Landon Ronald's 'Down in the Forest' which were played at twice the correct speed. Tom turned not a hair, but sang a little louder and with more emphasis, until the wandering pianist was brought back on course.

His wardrobe needed attention and a blue suit was ordered which would serve for concerts and special occasions. A reminder of the year was provided in the tailor's description of the colour. Coronation blue. Very popular, it seems, in the year when Edward VIII was due to be crowned, but while Tom got his suit, the king remained without a crown. Another date, but this time the programme was shared with Lorna Wood, a pianist who had just made her Aeolian Hall debut and Tom was pleased to be in such professional company for the Heaton Moor Methodist Guild. They chatted at the end of the concert about the 'musical profession'. Some of these engagements left him depressed. Stretford Methodist Church Annual Concert was one.

20th January 1937
Didn't have a very enthusiastic evening. The audience were unappreciative, although the place was more or less full. We tried our very best to keep the items interesting, but it was to no avail.

Occasionally there were unexpected difficulties as when the piano was covered in vegetables and fruit for the Harvest Festival and couldn't be moved. He had to sing with his accompanist's back towards him. Philosophically, he recorded it as *'another experience'*.

His interest in all kinds of music was developing rapidly and his regular attendance in the cheapest seats for the Hallé Orchestra was matched by frequent listening to the BBC. An event of enormous significance dominated the music world that year when Arturo Toscanini conducted the BBC Symphony Orchestra in a series of concerts. These were not to be missed. Nor too the Prague Philharmonic's visit to Manchester under Rafael Kubelik. One word summed up their performance: *'magnificent'*. Most evenings were filled with study. Two or three hours at the end of his working day was usual. *'Why can't I study during the day?'* he complained.

Money was always a concern, and increasingly so. An ice cream bought during the interval at a cinema cost 6d – six pence. *'Should have been 2d – tuppence – considering its small size.'* A ticket to hear Gigli at 6 shillings (equivalent price today would be £12) was money well spent. *'His magnificent voice filled the hall.'* He hurried to the Midland Hotel after the concert to get Gigli's autograph. It was a long wait, but he was rewarded.

Before the end of the year a young woman made an appearance who he describes as *'lovely'*. *'Yes, even more than that.'* He was obviously attracted to her, but the relationship didn't develop. Too many commitments; too much study; the music came first. It always would. Her name was H. Robertson, and the surname is one which would mean a great deal in years to come.

In August 1937 the country experienced a heat wave. Day after day of sunshine and soaring temperatures. Tom's temperature was soaring too, and a visit to Blackpool and the beaches did little to cool him. There seemed to be girls everywhere he looked: the swimming baths, the tennis court and the park, and several found their way into his diary. Not content with describing their hair and eyes, he comments on the dresses they wore. The colour of the material and the design; but Elsie, like Helen and Ann, even a beauty voted Manchester Railway Queen, were diversions for an hour or, at the most, an evening. There was too much to do: harmony exercises; counterpoint problems to solve; new songs to learn; important things like that. Admirable of course, but it was a very hot summer. His teeth were playing up and a visit to the dentist gave little cause to smile! Four to come out, four to be filled, he was told. Fortunately the extractions were from the back, but today's dentist would have saved them.

A visit to Wright Greaves' music shop and the purchase of three lectures on singing by Harry Plunkett-Greene was good value for a shilling, he thought. This was his bedtime reading at the time, but his opinion of the eminent teacher was mixed: *'I have doubts about this fellow,'* he writes. *'He advocated that interpretation is much more important than good tone emission. I don't agree. I say 50%/50%'.*

A good engagement at the Wagon and Horses Hotel for the bowling club's annual dinner allowed him to complete the payment of his suit which was ready for collection.

As the year came to an end he totalled up his engagements. A wedding here, a masonic ladies' night there. The fees ranged between 5/- and £1/5/-, and the total of £17/8/6 was little enough for a year's work, but his repertoire had increased considerably, and he had been heard by audiences at the Central Hall, Midland Hotel, Queen's Park Theatre and numerous churches in Manchester and its suburbs. Perhaps next year would be more profitable, but for the moment he was content.

At twenty-three the voice was maturing nicely. Christmas 1937 and even Tom could afford to relax and did so in good company.

25th December 1937

The party was very enjoyable and the best part was when we all relaxed and Hilda and I went into the front room and utilised the settee to the best advantage! She looked beautiful in a white satin frock with a tight fitting lace top and three quarter length sleeves made entirely by herself!

We hope he didn't worry too much about crushing it. Some days later Tom was overwhelmed with a desperate frustration concerning his job and the future. He wrote in a mood of urgency:

Sometimes the great desire to become a fine singer runs riot with my emotions. Just at the moment I feel like jumping off my stool in the office and rushing out to do something drastic. It isn't fame I long for, but the ability and knowledge of how to use my voice and how to interpret. I long to be trained by some very experienced teacher. I'm anxious to get amongst the right circle of people who can help me.

The Chance to Sing

While Tom rarely had any serious doubts about his future, or if he did, refused to entertain them for more than the briefest moment, by the end of 1938 he knew that he was on the way.

He was maturing rapidly and was proud of a fine physique. His weight had increased in the last year to 13$^1/_2$ stone, but it was evenly distributed over his 6 feet frame and he cut a splendid figure at the swimming pool and tennis courts. His voice was also developing, and every occasion when he sang was followed by complimentary notices.

He was well aware that his voice was unusually smooth and even throughout its range and now it was becoming increasingly powerful. He had some unconventional ways of testing this:

'Often, when I am walking along the road, a train or similar heavy vehicle making a considerable collection of noises will pass me. I then take the opportunity to compete with the noise and sing as though I was in some massive place. In common slang I let it rip! I do this mostly when I am going home in the evening from the office. I'm always glad to turn my back on the place....

He did appreciate one area of the office, however: the lavatories! He was fascinated by the acoustics there and made use of them.

Sometimes when I have been staying late alone I have sung to my heart's content while taking a wash. The voice seems to ring in every corner. I certainly have much easier control in comparison to singing at home, where there are several pieces of furniture and a carpet. I wish I had the opportunity of practising in a room with similar acoustics to those in the toilet!

Although he was well developed physically, he was conscious of a certain immaturity and felt that he was younger than his twenty-four years. This was to do with the ways of the world. From a spiritual viewpoint he was quite advanced:

It's in my very soul. In every part of me. That wonderful desire to be able to sing. To be an exponent of that art. In my own little world of inexperience it is my longing. To me it is life, understanding and satisfaction of aesthetic emotions. I want correctly adjusted motives and materialisation of sincere desire.

Phew! Well the language may be extravagant but the sentiments undoubtedly ring true. There is by this time a spiritual understanding rather than a religious zeal surprising in a young man of Tom's background. His appreciation of nature and the life-force within him testify to this. The voice belongs to him most certainly, but it is an instrument he is required to make use of, and consequently he has no choice but to work as hard as possible.

His lessons with Mr Evans had brought him a long way, but it was clear that the pupil had led the teacher, at least during the years since he had returned to singing. The engagements referred to previously had given him the confidence to face an audience, but the measure of his musical growth had been determined by the graded examinations of the Associated Board of the Royal Schools of Music and this year (1938) saw Tom's success at the highest level when he was awarded the Gold Medal.

From this point Tom regarded himself as a professional singer, and the joy he experienced in the visit to London to receive his medal from the Duke of Kent at St James' Palace is touchingly recorded in a notebook bought specially for this purpose. The food he ate in several West End restaurants was obviously superior to what he was used to, and he savoured every mouthful. The sights of the capital were viewed and appreciated with the enthusiasm of a schoolboy on an annual outing. But the moment when he received his medal topped it all:

15th July 1938

I shall never forget the intense silence as the Duke entered. We all rose of course and then we all sat again when he sat down.... At approximately 3.30 my name was called out and I walked up to the table where the Duke stood. I took hold of the medal with my left hand and shook his hand at the same time with the right. He then asked me one or two interesting questions concerning my singing and study. I answered him quite calmly and this was a surprise to me to be able to do so. I looked straight into his face as I spoke. It was a most wonderful moment for me. I couldn't realise that I was stood there speaking to him. Yet it was reality and the studying I have done and the perseverance seemed to be rewarded with the honour of that moment.

Mr Evans was allowed to accompany him into the palace (only one person for each candidate) and after the ceremony they joined his mother on the pavement outside. Her pride was that of any mother and the photographers were there to capture the event.

The evening was spent with friends in Pinner[*] and after the expected demands for him to sing were gratified Tom joined his friends in the garage for a game of darts. The others had begun and scored heavily, but Tom finished the day in style.

I joined in surreptitiously and would you believe it, I won.

The following year (1939) marked the beginning of Tom's professional life and it was illustrated by his withdrawal from the cast of the Refuge Assurance Company's production of *The Rainbow Inn*. He liked neither the music nor the libretto, and one

---

[*] Pinner will feature in his life fifteen years later as the location of his home. Coincidence, or did Tom make a note for the future?

more engagement was no longer sufficient reason to sing. He wrote to the Society's secretary accordingly. We can assume they were displeased and probably thought he was getting above himself.

Internationally, the situation was worsening by the day, and Chamberlain and Halifax were leaving for talks with Mussolini and Ciarri in Rome. Tom hoped for a successful outcome but things looked grim. As if the European news was not bad enough, there were problems closer to home and three bombs were exploded in Manchester. An IRA unit was held responsible, but no-one was reported killed or injured and life went on. Later reports stated that one man had died.

Grateful though he was for Mr Evans' instruction, it was time to make a move, and Tom applied for entry to the Royal Manchester College of Music[*], where the eminent bass Norman Allin was a professor. He hoped the local education committee would grant him a scholarship to study there, but he was uncertain of getting the necessary assistance. Feeling reasonably confident, Tom went to the college for an audition and sang for Allin. He was also given exercises to test his ear. Dr Brearley was in charge of this class and was very complimentary. Norman Allin was extremely impressed with the young tenor and told him what a fine voice he had. 'Some tightness, due no doubt to nerves,' was Allin's only criticism.

More engagements were offered following the publicity about the gold medal: some close to Manchester; but others farther afield. He was asked to state his terms, and he began to quote in line with other performers at the beginning of their careers. He accepted engagements in Bolton, Pendleton, Stockport and Jersey. Unlike many singers, Tom's interest in music was extensive and not confined to vocal music. His evenings were spent listening to concerts broadcast by the BBC, and as often as not it was instrumental and orchestral music which attracted him. Brahms' symphonies were among his favourites at this stage.

He attended the Hallé concerts whenever he could and this year

---

[*] Tom's teachers at the Royal Manchester College were Harold Dawber – Harmony, Norman Allin – Singing, Miss Annie Lord – Piano, Dr Herman Brearley – Music Dictation and Sight Singing.

was memorable, with visits by two of the world's greatest conductors to Britain: Weingartner to Manchester and Toscanini to London, as the guest of the BBC Symphony Orchestra. The Italian maestro's interpretations were electrifying and the BBC orchestra played as if possessed. Tom sat with his ear glued to the wireless and was stunned by the music, much of which he was hearing for the first time. He knew the instruments of the orchestra and could distinguish which were playing in the most richly orchestrated passages.

Apart from the music, there was something in the air and Tom sensed it. Always a film fan, he loved the new releases and was thrilled by Errol Flynn as Robin Hood which was showing at the Deansgate Cinema. One or two girls were occupying his thoughts and Elsie and Millie were more than willing to hold his hand in the cinema, or cuddle on a park bench, however cold the weather, but Tom kept his emotions tightly under control and the spirit of the times plus his religious convictions prevented any unwanted complications. All very frustrating no doubt, but necessary if his musical ambitions were to be realised, and that seemed quite possible in the magical year of 1939.

In February he heard Elgar's *Dream of Gerontius* under Dr Malcolm Sargent at a Hallé concert.

9th February 1939

Hurried home at 5.30 to have tea and change and went to the Hallé to hear the 'Dream of Gerontius'. Heddle Nash as Gerontius, Gladys Ripley as the Angel, and Harold Williams as the Priest. This is the first time I have heard this work and I was very much impressed... I admired Nash's musicianship, for he sang the whole work without a copy and made no mistakes.... I'm afraid Nash's singing tone was stringy and thin at times!

Tom cannot have realised that of all the works he would hear this was the one with which he would become most closely identified. A favourite of Heddle Nash, who took over the rôle from Gervase Elwes, the original Gerontius, but those who heard both admired Nash's interpretation more and Tom certainly learned a great deal from him. Other comparisons must wait until later in our story.

For the moment his daily routine remained the same. Monday to Friday stuck to his desk at the CPA. Lunchtime walks with Ken. Evenings for study. The weekends for church and relaxation.

No news came from the Manchester College, and the Education Committee was bogged down with hundreds of applications. Some consolation was supplied by Millie; and Wendy Hiller was starring in *Pygmalion* at the Paramount Cinema.

When not studying or singing, Tom was busy promoting himself. Some business cards with *Gold Medallist* were printed and with these he made a point of seeing people who might be helpful, and was not slow to call on theatre managers when there was a chance of getting an engagement. The organist of the Paramount was advertising for good artists to appear with him and Tom went backstage during the interval. Money was never his chief concern. Just as important was the building of a reputation and he was happy to sing in several concerts when there was no fee, for the chance of a review in the Manchester *Guardian*. One day Tom would be every agent's ideal artist: the kind who sees his career as something growing day by day; never missing an opportunity; the career always coming first.

Tom was not only physically strong but a natural sportsman. If he hadn't been blessed with a remarkable voice he might have set his sights on playing cricket for Lancashire or maybe Glamorgan. He was admiring when introduced to the great Len Hutton, two years Tom's junior, but already a name to conjure with. When he played for the firm he was successful and scored more runs than anyone else. At the tennis club he made a name for himself, but there were a few raised eyebrows when his desire to win seemed too intense for a social occasion. Throughout his life there would only be one way to do things – as well as possible. It was not a question of being better than someone else; that might or might not be the case, and Tom was the most generous of artists. It was merely in the doing of the thing required. Be it the singing of an aria, or the return of a powerful service, he had to give one hundred per cent and nothing less.

While awaiting news from the college Tom contacted the Royal

Academy and Royal College in London. In fact he would have loved to go to London, but the problems of living there were too difficult to surmount and he suspected that any grant from Manchester would be linked with his attending the local college. In the event, the long awaited news arrived and both the place at college and the grant attached were his for the taking. He had a few weeks to hand in his notice to the CPA and prepare himself for what he had longed for; a full time course at the Royal Manchester College of Music starting on the 27th September 1939.

In June, Tom was browsing through the journals in his local newsagent's shop when he picked up a copy of Picture Post, the most popular magazine of the day and a forerunner in the field of photo journalism. Something caught his eye.

19th June 1939

A weekly periodical called "Picture Post" contains a very interesting article about the now famous opera house at Glyndebourne. The theatre has been built in the beautiful grounds of John Christie's wonderful home on the banks of the river Bourne in Sussex. The price of the seats are 35/- and 40/-. The height of society attend and great artists are engaged – at least 50% of them English. There is a broadcast from Glyndebourne next Wednesday. Dino Borgioli is in the cast!

and two days later

21st June 1939

Listened to Don Giovanni from Glyndebourne. Borgioli was to have sung Don Ottavio, however for some reason he was unable to, and David Lloyd substituted. He sang very well, especially the famous aria 'Il mio tesoro'. Brownwell was Don Giovanni. I think that this fellow is one of the greatest operatic baritones of today!

Many music lovers were now listening to the relays from Glyndebourne, but few could have listened with such attention, and even fewer who would one day command that particular stage themselves.

Anxious to learn more about the singer's art (and by this time knowledge of microphone technique was an important part) Tom attended studio performances in Manchester whenever he could and seems to have been as interested in the positioning of the microphones and the singers' relationship to them as in the singing itself.

Tom was preparing for the studio himself with a BBC audition, and he decided to extend his repertoire of songs with music by Roger Quilter. One particularly appealed to him.

I have been given a copy of Quilter's 'Go Lovely Rose' and find it a lovely song. Simple but appealing. There is no beating about the bush. The message is so clear.

A broadcast of operatic arias by Dino Borgioli was announced in the Radio Times and Tom made a note in his diary not to miss it. He admired Borgioli greatly and planned to write to him. The distinguished tenor was more than kind on the one occasion when they met and spent several minutes talking to and encouraging him.

Tom generally confined his reading to books on music and was enthusiastic about the biography of the Welsh singer, David Ffrangcon Davies which had just been published.

I am finding it very interesting to read how his boyish ambitions were eventually realised. Some are synonymous with my own!

His mother's health was indifferent at this time and Tom was much concerned. A move to another house was under consideration, a move that would bring the two families: Mary and Thomas, with Tom; and their daughter Vera and husband David Edwards together under one roof. This was precipitated by the probability of war, for Baden Street was in a far from safe area and there was another important family member to consider, little Gwyneth, the Edwards' ten-year-old and a favourite of Tom's.

Tom was irritated that the decision to move had been postponed several times, because his mother and Vera couldn't make up their minds. His father was not involved. The women could do what they pleased in his view. Finally the move took place and 18 Essex Road became home to the six of them.

News of the Royal visit to the United States and Canada by

King George and Queen Elizabeth vied for space in the newspapers with the Spanish Civil War, but it was no contest so far as Tom was concerned. A patriot at heart, his meeting with the Duke of Kent had captured his loyalty forever.

Nevertheless the Spanish news was disquieting, with talk of conscription for young men between the ages of twenty and twenty-one hard to shrug off. He refused to worry however, dismissing the politics of Spain or Germany as a silly game: a game that would certainly not interfere with his plans for the future.

The broadcasts which claimed his attention at this time included Toscanini with the BBC Symphony Orchestra in Beethoven's Fifth:

I enjoyed the performance and am grateful for the chance to hear such events in London's musical life, but I am not really satisfied. I would prefer to receive the whole balance of the tone perfectly and not through a microphone.

Life at the office went on much the same, but there was a big difference now that his days there were numbered. Occasionally, perhaps, he looked at his colleagues and tried to imagine how he would feel if this was all he could look forward to. No doubt he shuddered at the thought. Certainly the prospect of war was horrifying to contemplate – but the awful boredom of the CPA and a lifetime as a clerk surrounded by the inane chit-chat of his co-workers was dreadful in another sense.

If I once become the singer I want to be, I will never waste time..... Every day provides the opportunity for advancement as a musician and a human being. Not to grab each moment and put it to full use is immoral!

The engagements at St John's, Pendleton and Kings Hall, Bolton were worthwhile in several ways.

1st April 1939
Pendleton was a very good concert of a high standard with only one or two blemishes. Several people were kind in expressing their appreciation of my singing. The evening was more interesting too because M. Charles came.

Tom was inclined to use an initial and surname when writing about a girl who was potentially important to him. It was a sure sign of his romantic interest.

That summer Tom told Millie that he loved her and received her assurances that she felt the same. Why nothing came of it we do not know. A move from Manchester? Another man (less serious if not so good looking)? Another girl (more involved with music)? These are a few possibilities. Certainly another girl was mentioned, and was given that intriguing initial and surname.

Tom's attendance at the Hallé's concerts brought him into contact with several girls who were already students at the College. He also attended the Open Practice recitals, which were part of the College's programme to provide a platform for promising students and it was at one of these that he met M. Lingard. In fact they'd met a couple of years before when she played the flute at a church concert, but she was only Mary then. Now, they were both studying music seriously and this girl had many desirable qualities. She was pretty and vivacious, and the daughter of one of Manchester's notable musicians – Joseph Lingard, first flute in the Hallé – and she received complimentary tickets for concerts which she occasionally passed to Tom! If one adds to this her name, which was the same as his mother's....

From early on Tom had clear ideas of what he would like to find in a wife. In a notebook used for planning he wrote under his life objectives:

Life with a definite objective is inevitably exciting. To be diligent and assiduous towards the materialisation of that objective is my aim. To develop intellectually and obtain my Mus. Doc. To find a wife who is also intellectual and with a deep interest in music. She must be able to play an instrument and to criticise intelligently on tone, rhythm, efficacy of performance etc.

Here we go again with the earnestness seen throughout his life. Judging by the language used, we may be grateful Tom did not consider a writer's career.

If Tom's father took a back seat in many of the day to day decisions at Essex Road, it was not because he had nothing to say, but rather because he was tired out from working on the railway. His job as coachman may not have been the hardest in physical terms, but the hours were long and when not dealing with the horses and carriage which were a legacy of Victorian times, he was given other work to do. The result was that the home was run entirely by Mary and he kept out of what didn't concern him. On the other hand, his interest in Tom was unwavering, and his love of singing and the career that some people spoke about was a source of great pride. If Thomas Thomas had to work all the hours God sent, then he was prepared to do so.

He sat quietly on many a Sunday evening listening intently to his son accompanied by Vera, and his opinion was respected however simple the remark. Tom was always prepared to hear criticism provided he respected the person it came from and the comment was made on purely musical grounds.

Around this time Tom received a letter from Edward Isaacs, who ran Manchester's Tuesday mid-day recitals.

A nice letter set in a considerate way. He (Isaacs) advised me to wait until I've been to College and gained wider experience before appearing, because there is such a high standard required. After reading his letter I'm convinced he's correct.

The gold medal of the Associated Board was his, but it hadn't gone to his head. How to get wider experience was the problem and he wouldn't be finished at the College for three years. This was the sort of situation where some practical advice came in handy. His father provided it. 'It's not what you know, but who you know that counts.' Obvious enough, so let him get his notebook out and plan his next moves. He heads the page *Sources to Try*.

Daily Express
A Gramophone Company
Landon Ronald (distinguished conductor)

Religious Film Society
Isobel Baillie
Harris Sellick
Clifton Helliwell
Mathewson Watson

A mixed list of organisations and people who might be able to help. He must write to them all. As time would show, it seems he did.

But now Bolton's King's Hall took priority and a performance of Maunder's *From Olivet to Calvary*. He shared the stage with a baritone whose fine voice was not matched by his musicianship. *'He could have treated the words more tenderly,'* Tom complains.

He rarely criticised those things in a voice over which the singer has no control. Blessed with a splendid instrument himself, he attached far more importance to questions of musicianship and those things which could be altered. His praise was frequently lavished on singers with modest voices, but whose intelligence and love for the language raised their performance to a level which could be called art.

Conflict 1939-1945

The weather that summer was wonderful, and Tom went to Birch Park to play tennis with Ken whenever he could. Sometimes they played doubles and one such game at the end of August was finished abruptly by dark clouds appearing as if from nowhere and thunder and lightning breaking the skies. Tom ran with his companions to shelter and shivered in his wet tennis clothes. Suddenly a premonition took hold that they would not be playing tennis much longer and just a week later, on 3rd September, war was declared.

On Saturday 23rd, Tom went to the CPA for the last time. Apart from one or two moments of sadness when saying goodbye to old colleagues Tom was in great spirits. So much so, that he felt obliged to curb his enthusiasm and behave quietly, insisting that his good-byes were in fact only cheerios and he would be keeping in touch.

Millie knew better but understood. She was feeling very sad, for she sensed that this was the end of more than Tom's job. A Blackbird fountain pen was her farewell present and she had placed it on his desk as he made the rounds. His nine hated years at the CPA were over and all he had longed for was waiting for him.

Tom must have looked at the chair he had occupied for so long with an emotion far removed from the contempt he had felt previously. As he glanced around at all the smiling faces he felt as if he were guilty of betrayal. A rat leaving a sinking ship. His confused feelings were not helped when he finally knocked on the manager's door. 'Good luck, Tom,' Mr Hilbert said. 'You're doing the right thing. In any case Calico Printers is a dead end. Not that I need to tell you that.'

The evening was a time for celebration, but strangely Tom wasn't in the mood. Following some supper at Lyons in Oldham Street he walked with Millie to their seat in Rycroft Park and tried to console her. He suddenly realised he was consoling himself.

Four days later Tom entered the doors of the Royal Manchester College of Music as a full time student.

His first lesson was with Norman Allin. He sang 'When the Stars were Brightly Shining' from *Tosca* and waited for Allin's comments nervously. 'You've an excellent voice, but there's a tendency to go back into the throat. Not to worry. I'll give you some exercises which will help with that.' Allin added that Tom would need to study French, Italian and German. 'Absolutely essential,' he emphasised. How right he was. Italian caused him some unexpected problems later in his career.

James Bernard was his elocution teacher. R.J. Forbes was in charge of the opera class. Tom enjoyed this class enormously. The group sight read *Il Seraglio* and Tom was asked to sing Belmonte. Forbes was delighted and talked about the possibility of producing the opera at College.

Feeling part of things now he decided to buy a few items from the College 'shop': *One tie 3/11. One badge 1/-. One muffler 8/11.* His feelings were expressed in one word – *Gosh!*

At the end of the week a concert was to take place at Wesley Hall. Agnes Moseley – Soprano. Mary Lingard – Flute. Albert Knowles – Pianist. Cai Jones – Comic. Tom Thomas – Tenor. The presence of a comic at certain concerts was considered essential by the organisers if the audience were to be kept happy. Although Tom was disapproving of concert artists doing cabaret work – this was a come-down, he believed – he really enjoyed the comic Cai Jones, and believed he provided a sort of safety valve and that once the audience had had their laugh, their more serious natures could be appealed to. However it was, Mary was playing and Millie was in the audience, so it must have been an exhilarating evening for him.

Tom worked hard at the piano in preparation for his second

study lesson and a Mozart Sonata in G occupied some hours. Who would be teaching him had still to be settled, the second study being considered less important. In real terms it may have been, but, like everything else, Tom took it seriously. A change had come over him since leaving the office. Was it possible in just one week? This had to do with his attitude of mind, but not only that. His voice, too, seems to have responded to the new situation. On the Sunday following the Wesley Hall concert he sang at Alderley Edge Methodist Church. It was Harvest Festival and his final solo was 'Open the Gates of the Temple'. He sang from the pulpit and was suddenly aware that he had never sung so well before. His voice reached out and touched the hearts and minds of the congregation. It was as if God was working through his singing. The eyes of the men and women were misty. The children were spellbound. As Tom was also in tears, he made his way to the vestry rather than to his place in the choir stalls.

It is probable that this occasion marks a turning point in his career: the moment when the singer became an artist.

Perhaps Allin had noticed a change too, for a few lessons later he was concentrating on the solos from the *Messiah*. He seemed anxious to polish Tom's interpretations as quickly as possible. Was he preparing the young tenor for early professional exposure?

Without doubt Norman Allin recognised immediately that his new student had exceptional ability and, equally important, the purpose and dedication needed to reach the top. 'So back once more to "Thy Rebuke", and please, please omit the appogiaturas.'

It was decided that his piano teacher should be Miss Annie Lord and he played his Mozart Sonata for her. She criticised his technique, but approved his musicianship. 'We have to get those fingers working. It's very much hit and miss, isn't it?' Her manner was sharp, but Tom wasn't put off by this:

'She's impatient and not inclined to encourage, but I shall be all right with her...She is going to concentrate on my technique.'

Allin came to Manchester once every two weeks and gave his students a lesson on consecutive days. For his second and third lessons Tom sang in Italian and German.

Sang 'Che gelida manina' from 'La Bohème'. The top C was all right and he was pleased..... Mr Allin liked my singing in 'Breit über mein Haupt' by Richard Strauss. I think I am going to enjoy singing in German as much as I do Italian.

Working very hard and enjoying every minute, it was easy to forget the country was at war. So far it hadn't affected him much, and there were many exciting new things to occupy him. Some public meetings were announced and there was talk of it all being over in six months. The famous actress Dame Sybil Thorndike came to Manchester to plead for Christ's principles to be given a chance to resolve the international situation.

It was to be the most concentrated period in Tom's twenty-five years. Every morning for the first month he reminded himself that this was what he had been longing for. The chance to study, to immerse himself in music. The memory jogging was quite unnecessary, for no student worked harder and yet, perfectionist that he was, he always felt that he could have done more. Another page of harmony. Another hour at the piano. A better preparation for the high Bb in his singing lesson. Later, he relaxed a little and took everything in his stride, but he never ceased to feel gratitude for his good fortune and wondered just how long it would be before the war caught up with him.

Tom no longer entertained any thoughts that it might have been preferable to be a student at the Royal Academy or Royal College of Music. In any case, those ideas had been mainly to do with being in London and close to Covent Garden and Sadler's Wells. Within a short time he had become extremely proud of the Royal Manchester College of Music and knew that he was receiving a training second to none.

Two important concerts are recorded in the College Reports for 1940 and 1941 and both involve Tom. On the 28th May, 1940 he sang Vaughan Williams' *On Wenlock Edge*, and added to his repertoire a work that would stay with him throughout his career. Marjorie Thomas was a fellow student and had to pass through the hall while Tom was rehearsing. She remembers the impact of his voice as if it were yesterday. 'I was literally stopped in my tracks by the sound and the clarity of the words.'

The second concert mentioned was his last before call-up came. The Albert Hall in Manchester was the location and Tom sang extracts from Bach's *St. Matthew Passion*. Perhaps a suitable farewell for a soldier about to go to war.

Normal Allin felt very keenly the interruption that was bound to occur when his students were called up, and a recommendation from him to ENSA (Entertainments National Services Association) and the Carl Rosa Opera enabled Tom to gain some valuable experience during the first year of war, and before the conflict demanded the enrolment of his generation of 26 year olds. It was a taste of a career and tantalisingly sweet.

Tom's regiment was the Royal Corps of Signals and he found himself in Sand Hutton, Yorkshire, where he underwent his basic training. His comrades were mostly ex Post Office workers, the traditional recruitment for the Signals, and one became his best friend during the war and remained so for the rest of his life.

His nine years of employment by the CPA had given people a chance to get to know him and if there were some, and there undoubtedly were, who still thought him aloof, others recognised the signs of considerable shyness. Life for Tom was time. Precious time in which to get things done. To waste it was unthinkable. That many did not have a clearly defined goal was unfortunate but not really his problem. He did have and that meant living each day to the full. Planning the hours for work and recreation. Not leaving things to chance.

Richard Colclough may be regarded not only as a friend but also a fan. He told his wife, Beryl, about a walk they took through a forest close to Sand Hutton. Of the thrill of hearing Tom suddenly burst into song with a voice 'that was out of this world.' He could not believe his ears. 'I had never heard such a pure English voice.' These were his words as she recalls them and if the description failed to give credit to the Welsh genes, we know what he meant.

In fact Tom's voice was not what most people have in mind when they speak of a Welsh tenor. In speech his voice was touched by his parents' influence, but there were also strong Mancunian tones and these struggled under the discipline of a man concerned to speak well. One thing is certain. In the army he was always Tommy and never Taffy.

By this time Mary Lingard was his acknowledged girlfriend and the pen given to him by Millie wasn't used to write to her. Mary had also had to lay aside her flute and put on the blue-grey uniform of the Women's Auxiliary Air Force, and a posting to the Orkneys didn't make matters easier.

They had barely had time to adjust to this new schedule when Tom was posted to the Guards' Armoured Division in Ascot. Mary was devastated, but there were two consolations for Tom. The first was his proximity to London and what remained of its musical life. The second, the posting of Richard Colclough to similar duties. Nothing was certain in war time, and another posting could come without warning. In the event, Ascot was their base until 1942, when they were sent to St Paul's School (the H.Q. of General Mont-gomery) in Hammersmith. In the language of the day, it was the cushiest billet possible. Tom was recognised as a 'talent' by the officers of the regiment and sang for his supper on many social occasions when ladies were present. We can imagine the pleasure of his audience as they listened to the handsome young Signalman singing love songs in those anxiety-filled days.

As a reward Tom was given the special job of selecting suitable shows for the troops, and conscientiously sat through everything, in order to be able to recommend what he considered the boys would appreciate most. As his complimentary tickets came in pairs, Richard was his constant companion on these skirmishes in the West End.

Tom and Mary became engaged towards the end of the year and were married on 14th August 1943 at St Ann's Church in Man-chester.

Until the invasion their marriage would consist of hurried phone calls, longed for weekends – frequently cancelled at the last minute – and once during that period, ten days annual leave. Compared with many others they knew they were lucky.

Tom's luck held even after the invasion took place, but Richard was less fortunate and found himself in a different unit and actively involved in a series of difficult battles following the landing at Arromanches.

By contrast Tom was sent first to Rear HQ in Normandy and shortly afterwards to 21 Army Group Rear HQ in Brussels. He couldn't have done better had he planned it himself.

The war brought to an end so many hopes and plans that Tom felt something akin to guilt insofar as his own career was concerned. In fact while hostilities continued elsewhere, Tom was able to study at the Brussels Conservatoire, and once the armistice was signed he advanced his professional career with engagements in Brussels, Antwerp and Liège. As a British soldier he was very warmly received and he chose to sing Benjamin Britten's *Les Illuminations*. No evening clothes were needed for these appearances. His battle dress was brushed and pressed and served him admirably.

Someone to whom Tom was indebted for arranging his duties to allow him to attend the Conservatoire and undertake these concerts, was the ATS sergeant who was in charge of the office: Mary Cottle. A keen music lover, Mary had a soft spot for the young tenor in her section and did all she could to help him. Now Mary Kirkby, she recalls Tom's reserved manner and serious disposition. That was until the day when he received an invitation to sing for the Belgian Royal Family. This was the result of the music governess of the Royal children attending his concert with the Brussels Philharmonic, and her enthusiasm for his voice was boundless. The invitation which followed had Tom jumping around, and did him no end of good with his CO. With this kind of patronage any lingering doubts about his future vanished and Tom couldn't wait to return to Norman Allin and complete his studies.

One day when Tom was shopping at the *Bon Marché* which was quite close to the Signals' office in the Avenue Louise, he noticed a crowd in the book department and hurried over to see what was going on. He was delighted to find Diana Napier, the wife of the great Richard Tauber, busily signing copies of her auto-biography. This was too good an opportunity, even for the reticent young tenor, and he immediately got into conversation with the famous actress and told her about his hopes for the future. It could well have been the moment when he decided to act on something Norman Allin had said about his name being unsuitable for a concert career; at any rate, his next public appearance was as Richard Lewis.

Both names were part of his family history in so far as his paternal grandfather's name was Richard, and his mother's maiden name was Lewis. The coupling of the two seemed appropriate as a professional or stage name and the fact that one of his heroes was Richard Tauber may have clinched matters. Perhaps he had heard that Tauber had changed his name from Ernst Seifert for similar reasons, although there was more to the Tauber story than that.

Tom's regret, when soon after his invitation to sing at the Palace he was posted to Oslo, is understandable. Apart from the composer Edvard Grieg, Norway had few pretensions to musical prestige and Brussels did seem to be the more desirable place for a soldier with the right connections.

However, one of his best connections was the manager of the Brussels Philharmonic Orchestra, who lost no time in informing his colleague, manager of the Oslo Philharmonic, about Tom's performance of Britten's *Les Illuminations* and an engagement to sing the same work followed.

Oslo one day and Stockholm and Copenhagen the next? Not quite, but within a few months Tom had sung *Les Illuminations* in Stockholm, and another of Britten's compositions, the *Serenade for Tenor, Horn and Strings* in Copenhagen. For a Signalman on duty he was doing extraordinarily well, and, by the same token so was Benjamin Britten.

If Tom didn't sing for the Norwegian King Haakon while stationed in Oslo, he did meet an artist of the highest stature, and a Queen of Opera. Few singers have been so universally admired as the great Wagnerian soprano, Kirsten Flagstaad, who invited him to dine and quickly became a good and generous friend. Her interest and appreciation meant more to Tom than any number of crowned heads.

1946 started well with thirty days' leave and Tom set sail for England. Mary met him at Stalybridge with the car and they began the process of getting to know one another again. News of Tom's concerts in Belgium and Scandinavia had preceded him and consequently their second honeymoon was interrupted with an invitation to sing for Benjamin Britten and Rudolf Bing, then manager of Glyndebourne Opera. Any other interference with his precious leave would have been given short shrift, but an invitation of this kind was not to be missed.

We know where he auditioned: the Wigmore Hall. We know when: the 21st January. Unfortunately, we don't know what he sang, but we can guess. Some Mozart, probably. Some Handel, possibly. Some Britten without a doubt.

Understandably, Britten had been intrigued by the news of his music being performed in Europe by a serving soldier and wanted to hear for himself the young tenor responsible. In fact, Tom was no longer so young. The five years of war had brought him to his thirty-first year, but in terms of experience he was still at the beginning, and Britten was anxious to have confirmation of what he had been told.

By the end of the audition both the composer and Glyndebourne's manager knew that they had heard an exceptional talent of great promise.

In February he returned to Norway, but it would not be long before he was with Mary again, as they had planned to meet in Bergen where he was to sing next and to celebrate her release from the WAAF. Far from being upset by his musical activities, Tom's CO was proud that one of his men had talent useful at a diplomatic level, and the birthday of the British Consul was just such an occasion. After the concert Signalman Thomas was introduced to the Norwegian Foreign Minister and offered a glass of champagne as they chatted together. Ardwick and the CPA seemed a lifetime away, and Thomas Thomas, who was sometimes Richard Lewis, was beginning to realise his dream.

Arbeiderbladet (Oslo) 25/9/45
Richard Lewis – The Culture Vocalist
'The vocal concert performed by the English star singer Richard Lewis in the Aula on Friday proved to be a perfect festive hour. One half of the programme turned out to be a

musico-historical synthesis of Italian and German classicism. Scarlatti, Adolf Hasse, Pergolesi, Bach, Händel, Mozart and Donizetti were all recited by a vocal art which is of such universal proportions that it may express absolutely everything which the human voice is capable of interpreting within the bounds of musical art. Such an instrumental superiority which this precious throat represents has not been experienced in the Aula before in regard to male star singers. It may seem incredible, but it is nevertheless a fact, that all the classic, well-known gems, which embrace the most exacting tests of intonation, egality of all registers, breath technique, recitation, tone volume, interval assuredness, and passage colouring, in short anything within the bounds of technical proficiency which may be anticipated – all this was bent in under a musical ability and such a pure and noble spirit, that the audience was elevated into a superiorly spiritual sphere. ...

The audience left this concert with a feeling of having experienced something overwhelmingly magnificent. The applause and enthusiasm which increased into ovations do not suffice here. A profound reverence was left in the depth of one's soul.'

There was to be one further posting for Tom before his demobilisation came and this time it was to Germany. More precisely, to Hamburg.

Each move in his military career had brought an unexpected reward and his last months in Germany were no exception. Apart from several concert appearances, Tom was introduced to the eminent singing teacher, Professor Pacho Kochen and was able to have some lessons with him. Although they were few in number, Tom believed they were among his most influential musical experiences.

As a child Tom had been pleased to have the same name as his father, in spite of the teasing of other children who could not resist making fun of a classmate whose first and last names were the same. Tom, Tom, the piper's son.... We can imagine the sort of teasing to which he may have been subjected. We may also ask was he doing something more than simply choosing a suitable stage name when he became Richard Lewis?

Certainly Tom felt no shame about his origins, but in the more class-conscious society of the time a movement from working class to middle class was less easily negotiated and it may have been this social hiatus which gave rise to the aloofness which many observed. It is possible that psychologically a new name was needed to enter a new world; a kind of rebirthing; but, as with everything Tom did it was all or nothing, and consequently he confirmed his choice by deed poll once his demob papers came through. Poor Mary! Having just got used to being Mrs. Thomas, she now became Mrs. Lewis. Where would it end?

New Beginnings

Civvy Street for Richard meant the resumption of his studies, and again he was fortunate, for his professor at the Royal Manchester College of Music, Norman Allin, was also on the staff of the Royal Academy in London, and London was where he now needed to be. His only real concern therefore was that the Academy would accept him, and that the balance of his scholarship which had been provided by Manchester would be available for study in London.

Within a week, thanks largely to Allin, both matters were resolved and with a new 'service' flat (made available to ex-service-men and not a de luxe residence as the name suggests) Richard and Mary set up home. He began his studies on 23rd January 1947 with a history class in the morning and opera in the afternoon.

One of the conditions of their tenancy at Belsize Park Gardens was that no babies were allowed; however a baby of a different kind was, and without pondering the expense too much, Richard immediately purchased a Challen baby grand piano for £140. His careful economies and the fees for concerts in Europe during the last six months had provided a tidy bank balance, and compared to most couples they were comfortably off.

For an instrumentalist at the leading music schools, one of the major problems is combining the necessary attendance at class and orchestra with opportunities for professional work, and permission to be absent is not always granted. The young singer is in a different position, as voices of quality are so prized that, given the encouragement of one's professor, ways are found to allow the student to take advantage of any offers that come his way.

Richard's singing for Benjamin Britten a year earlier had not been forgotten, and now Richard found himself auditioning again, and then receiving an invitation to Britten's home in Oxford Square. To be given the chance to sing for the leading young composer in England, when that composer was devoted to another young tenor, Peter Pears, was special to say the least; but Richard Lewis had a lot going for him and he blessed the long evenings of study on the dining room table in Ardwick. All those harmony exercises and counterpoint. All those hours at the piano were about to pay off, for Richard had not only a voice in a million, but the musical knowledge and intelligence to learn new and dauntingly difficult music in a fraction of the time required by others. He recalled the invitations to parties which he had refused in favour of work. Sometimes, then, he had sighed; now he could afford to smile.

Britten could not have been more charming or more generous. The English Opera Group would be presenting *The Rape of Lucretia* and *Albert Herring*, and Britten wished him to sing the Male Chorus in the first and to share the part of Albert with Peter Pears in the second.

He was asked to supper the following evening, and joined a group which included Joan Cross, the Rt. Hon. Oliver Littleton, Karl Rankl and David Webster.

Peter Pears was there, of course and Britten played over the first act of *Albert Herring*. It was a memorable evening and Richard felt the glow of acceptance and success around the corner. The buses were running again following the strike, or he could have taken a cab, but he was happy to walk home, savouring the opportunity he had been given and considering what it could mean.

He didn't have long to wait. Just two weeks later the conductor Herbert Menges was on the phone. Peter Pears would not be able to sing in Britten's *Serenade* the following evening due to laryngitis and was it possible for him to take on the concert at such short notice?' This was Richard's first fully professional concert (22.3.47) in England – his *Messiah* appearances before the war in and around Manchester were hardly in the same league – and that evening the

Brighton Dome resounded to Richard's voice in duet with the greatest horn player of his generation, Dennis Brain. Menges was delighted.

Back to the Academy for his regular lessons, but mid-week he had an audition at the BBC. Many students would have taken the day off, if not the week – but not Richard. This was not his way. After all, he might learn the very thing that he would need one day and since the audition was at ten-thirty a.m., he could just make it back for the Sonata Recital (given by a young pianist he barely knew) at twelve. In any case some students from the Brussels Conservatoire were giving a concert in the afternoon and he owed a lot to Brussels.

A successful audition for the BBC generally meant a long wait for an engagement, even in those less-pressured days immediately after the war, but something of the impact that Richard's voice was having on the musical establishment may be gathered when we learn that he sang, in a broadcast performance a month later, Stravinsky's *Les Noces* under Walter Goehr. In between there was an invitation to sing in a Remembrance Day Concert in The Hague when Richard was presented to Princess Juliana and Prince Bernhard. An overnight stay with the Hope-Johnsons (Philip H-J the British Council representative in the Netherlands), was welcome and the excellent hospitality contrasted with the restrictions still in force at home.

Back to London; and alternating between the Academy and the real world of music, where he was a valued colleague of some of the most important artists in the country, was a difficult balancing act. Thus Norman Allin remained Mr Allin, but Britten and Pears were simply Ben and Peter. Another reason, possibly, for the aloofness in Richard's character was his wish to behave appropriately with everyone he met: rich and poor; famous and unknown. It would have required a quite different education to fit him for the world in which he now moved, and even those who had enjoyed that kind of education frequently got it wrong. All in all, Richard Lewis was doing quite well.

Rehearsals at Ben's Oxford Square house were exciting beyond his wildest imaginings. Here it was that conductor and chosen soloists came to know *Albert Herring* as Britten played the completed work to them. Getting to grips with the opera as a whole before rehearsals proper began. Finding his way into the mind of the character while learning music unknown to anyone. This was the sort of adventure he had always longed for.

The other opera, *The Rape of Lucretia*, in which he would sing the Male Chorus, also had to be learned, but he lapped it up. He was thirty-three and there was no time to be lost. The Academy term was well under way and he regarded his attendance at lessons as an obligation of the first importance. Norman Allin tentatively suggested he should take his Academy work a little less seriously in view of his professional commitments, but this was rejected by Richard. You either did things a hundred per cent, or not at all. Somehow he coped, but looking back later, he wondered how.

The English Opera Group was booked to open the season at the Royal Opera House, Covent Garden on 8th October, but before that there would be performances at Glyndebourne, a tour of the Netherlands and Switzerland and, finally, a week at the Theatre Royal, Newcastle.

It must be said that Richard's relationship with Britten was sometimes strained, for the composer was faced with a dilemma that could not easily be overcome. On the one hand, his partner in life, Peter Pears, was a highly gifted musician with a modest voice. On the other, Richard was every bit as musically accomplished, if not more so, and possessed of the finest voice in the land. For Britten the musician, the choice would have been clear-cut, but he was a man in love and inevitably there were other considerations.

Richard's first performance at Covent Garden, took place on 10th October 1947 when he sang the Male Chorus in *The Rape of Lucretia*. It went well and the press reviews were good. Richard was satisfied, all things considered. That he must have been nervous goes without saying. What did find its way into the margin of his diary was the fee for the performance – £28.

It had been a year to remember, but it was not over yet. On 21st October the postman brought a letter from London's second opera company, Sadler's Wells, offering him the part of Ferrando in Mozart's *Così fan Tutte*, and hardly had he finished reading it, when a telephone call came from David Webster, Director of the Royal Opera House, asking him to come into the office to discuss singing Peter in Britten's *Peter Grimes*. Was it possible that so much had happened so quickly? Reviewing the year Richard was overwhelmed with gratitude. He was convinced that none of the good fortune had happened by chance; that it was in answer to his prayers and his dedication. He believed God's hand was clearly to be seen, and he knew that Mary had also played her part at home in the success that was his.

Richard sang Peter Grimes at Covent Garden for the first time on 28th November 1947. An example of the reviews the next morning is the following:

> 'Richard Lewis gave a very moving performance of the name part. His voice is clear, his diction unforced, he has an excellent dramatic sense and is altogether a great gain to the cast of the opera. The whole performance was better co-ordinated than on the opening night.'
>
> S. G. in *The News Chronicle* 29.11.47

In the audience that night was Wilfred Stiff, general manager of the Liverpool Philharmonic Orchestra, who was spending a few days in London. Stiff had gone to Covent Garden expecting to hear Peter Pears in the part and remembers how impressed he was. 'I knew at once that this was a tenor of exceptional quality, combining a wonderful voice with real musicianship. At that time we had an outstanding group of singers who appeared regularly with the Orchestra. Elsie Morison, Kathleen Ferrier, Norma Proctor, Norman Walker, Owen Brannigan. I made a note to include Richard Lewis at the earliest opportunity.' December passed in a flash with more performances of *Grimes* and rehearsals for *Così fan Tutte* at Sadler's Wells.

After all their efforts, Richard and Mary were determined to make the most of Christmas and left for Manchester on the 23rd. Christmas dinner would be at Essex Road and in the evening they were going to Mary's parents. Richard longed to rest but knew there would be questions from all sides. He stretched his long legs in front of him and smiled contentedly. Mary said something, but he was asleep before the train left Euston.

A Family Man

As the stages in the development of an opera singer may be marked by the repertoire he sings, for his wife the career may be signposted more in terms of where they lived.

For Mary Lewis the early years were filled with change. In the space of eighteen months they moved from Belsize Park to Stanmore, and then to Pinner. Pinner must have made a favourable impression on Richard when he stayed there in 1938 – the evening of the Gold Medal presentation – for he referred to it several times in the intervening years. In fact they stayed there for nine years until they bought the house in Rickmansworth.

Mary recalls those days at 11 The Glen, Village Way, with a certain wistfulness. It seemed that anything was possible then. The phone rang constantly and the old theatrical adage that you're only as good as your last engagement was holding true for her husband. The thing was, Richard wasn't just good, he was very good indeed. Of course the voice was always remarkable; a beautiful instrument in every way; but it wasn't just the voice, it was also the man. Better looking with each year and still as dedicated and painstaking as he had been at the beginning. So many artists become complacent with success, but not Richard. Believing as he did that what he had been given was a gift from God, he was just as certain that the gift could be taken away.

Another factor to be considered was the negligible amount of stage training he had received. Apart from the advice of his teachers, and the brief experience with the Carl Rosa Opera Company, the only preparation he had been given were some stagecraft classes with Joan Cross. Every operatic performance demanded a considerable acting skill to make the character come alive, and if the singer was not required to engage in the subtle techniques of the Old Vic, nevertheless a polished characterisation was demanded. That Richard was able to satisfy these demands at Covent Garden and Sadler's Wells in spite of limited training, was in consequence of his natural stage gifts; and his competence as an actor was exchanged within a very few years for a wide-ranging authority.

And so it was left to Mary to provide not simply the comforts of home, but also the encouragement and understanding needed to see him through those testing days. She says he was an affectionate and caring husband, but there was a sharp edge to his tongue, and he could be extremely critical of those around him. On occasion, he spoke harshly and hastily, and then bitterly regretted what he had said. After these incidents he would be filled with remorse and tried desperately to make amends.

It is one thing to make a name in the opera house, it is quite another to build a reputation in the concert hall, but Richard had been waiting a long time for his chance and he was not about to ruin it. His year at the Academy had been valuable, but now he had to concentrate on the career, and reluctantly he called a halt to his studies.

The Liverpool Philharmonic was playing Beethoven's *Missa Solemnis* under Sir Malcolm Sargent and a tenor was required. Wilfred Stiff's memo, scribbled during the evening of Richard's debut in *Peter Grimes* a few months before was hardly needed. In response to the question 'Do you know the work?' Richard replied that he did, as he would do so often in the years to come. This was not the time to hum and ha. What he didn't know he would learn. And learn he did. On a train. In a plane. It made little difference where he was; his absorption of the score was uncanny. Many a conductor would have been delighted to learn so quickly. Stiff sums it up: 'Richard was a genius in his own way and able to take on board at sight all the elements of a composition.' His audition for Sargent was a hurried affair. 'Get round to Albert Hall Mansions at once,' he was told. Richard left, score in hand. Within the hour,

Sargent was on the phone with the briefest instruction: 'Book him.' Stiff now smiles as he recalls the conductor's enthusiasm.

Sargent was one of two British conductors who regarded Richard as 'first choice' when it came to certain works, and it is interesting that they could hardly have been more different in their musical approach. The other was Sir John Barbirolli.

Richard owed this introduction to his father-in-law, Joe Lingard, who played the flute for many years with the Hallé Orchestra. No doubt he would have been spotted soon enough, particularly as a son of Manchester, but it was a tip from Mary's father which led to his first engagement with the orchestra. Lady Barbirolli – the distinguished oboist, Evelyn Rothwell – remembers her husband's regard for the young tenor who kept himself to himself off stage, but was a changed man the moment he stepped onto the platform. This reserve, which was part of the essential Richard, might have been more easily understood a few years later, when actors like Clift and Brando turned it to their advantage. To sing for JB and the Hallé Orchestra was an occasion to be savoured. Perhaps some of his old friends like Ken were there. We can't be sure, but we do know that Richard gave a magnificent performance in Berlioz' *Childhood of Christ*, and so began his special relationship with Barbirolli.

It was at this concert that Richard first claimed the attention of the young music journalist Michael Kennedy. Almost fifty years later, the noted author of many books on music recalls following Richard's career with great interest, and picks out his Troilus, and Mark in *The Midsummer Marriage* as memorable. Of his Gerontius, Michael Kennedy is adamant that none has since come near to him. One of those early Elgar performances prompted the following letter:

16.x.50

Dear Richard Lewis
    Ever since Gerontius at Leeds I have been wanting to send you a word, but have not had a moment until now. I was really deeply touched by your singing of the part, and although of course it will mature in time, I do feel you

have it in you to become one of the finest Gerontius's of
your generation. It was very deeply sensitive and musi-
cianly, and I only beg you now to look after yourself, and
travel the paths of devotion and seriousness to your work
which I fear you have, and your reward should be great.
Yours very sincerely
John Barbirolli

With Covent Garden and Sadler's Wells employing him, Richard might well have regarded an audition for Glyndebourne as unwarranted, but the prestigious Sussex opera company had always occupied a special place in his mind and an invitation to sing for Moran Caplat was not to be ignored. Richard's unfailing musical judgement probably told him that this was just the setting where his voice would be heard at its best.

The year ahead looked forbidding in terms of the sheer volume of work lined up. How would his voice stand up to it? This was an unknown quantity at this early stage in Richard's career. He was still young and healthy and blessed with a robust physique and, perhaps even more important, a strong temperament. Nevertheless, the most experienced singer can run into trouble and a brilliant reputation be undone all too quickly. Nothing for it but to pray to God and put his trust in Him. How many times did Richard think those words during the remaining months of 1948? His diary indicates that he did so frequently, and certainly the schedule would have concerned the most seasoned artist.

Place	*Work*	*Number of Performances*
R.O.H. Covent Garden	*Peter Grimes*	*12*
Sadler's Wells Theatre	*Così fan Tutte*	*10*
Sadler's Wells in Manchester	*Così fan Tutte*	*2*
Glyndebourne Opera in Bath	*Il Seraglio*	*6*
R.O.H. Covent Garden	*Boris Godunov*	*5*
English Opera Group	*Albert Herring*	*12*
In various theatres on tour		
R.O.H. Cov. Gdn. in Brussels –		
La Monnaie	*Peter Grimes*	*2*

R.O.H. Cov. Gdn. at Paris Opera	*Peter Grimes*	*2*
Glyndebourne Opera Edinburgh Festival	*Don Giovanni*	*9*
BBC	*La Vida Breve*	*1*
Cambridge Festival	*Idomeneo*	*1*
BBC	*The Rescue*	*2*
BBC	*The Midsummer Marriage*	*1*
Plus Concerts:		
Newcastle Cathedral	*St. John Passion*	*1*
Oxford Festival	*Serenade*	*1*
Various: Manchester, Newcastle, Derby,		
Wolverhampton	*Messiah*	*4*
Broadcasts cont:	*B Minor Mass*	*3*
BBC R.P.O. Beecham	*The Seasons*	*6*
Plus recording:		
Decca	*Various*	

In addition to all the performances listed above, the hundreds of rehearsal hours involved, not to mention the travel undertaken represents an incredible effort. These works were all new to Richard and the stress of this must have been considerable, and yet apart from one week's holiday at the Woodland's Hotel in Sidmouth, there were only nineteen free days without rehearsal, or performance, or travel, or all three. When we are engaged in creative work which we love, there is clearly a level of energy available to us which keeps sickness at bay and enables us to accomplish an exceptional work load; however Richard set himself a task which few artists would consider reasonable, and came through with flying colours. It was a sign of his dedication and resolve that he never missed an engagement during this time, but as Mary had to content herself with that one week in Sidmouth, we may understand why her mind turned increasingly towards thoughts of a baby and the companionship of a child.

In 1949, just when everything he had hoped for was coming his way, Richard received the news that his father had died. He was singing *Peter Grimes* at Covent Garden and the management had been informed before the curtain went up, but understandably told Richard only after the performance. He was devastated. His last meeting with his father had taken place at London Road station where he had been changing trains while on tour and he carried with him for the rest of his life that memory of his father growing smaller and smaller as he waved him goodbye from the platform. In fact it had crossed his mind that this was possibly the last time they would meet. Some weeks later Richard sang his first *Messiah* with the Hallé and looked down to see his family sitting in a row with one empty seat next to his mother. This would have been heartbreaking for anyone, and no doubt Richard felt his loss keenly, but according to reports he sang superbly and his 'Comfort Ye' was memorable. Surely Thomas was listening.

The move from Stanmore to Pinner was left very much in Mary's hands, as Richard was constantly occupied with rehearsals and performances, and if his second year at Covent Garden was easier due to his increased experience, he was now much in demand for concerts and recitals.

A tour of Austria under the auspices of the British Council was a great success and culminated in recitals at the Salzburg *Mozarteum* and in Vienna. The concerts were broadcast and the reviews were good for a British singer who was being compared with the best in Europe.

Richard's meticulous preparation left nothing to chance and in his diary he notes that he must study *The Apostles*; *Gerontius*; *Te Deum*; *Magic Flute*; *Wenlock Edge*; *St. Matthew Passion*. All due for performance in the coming months. At the bottom of the page the single word *'spectacles'* indicated some new ones were needed. How the performers of the fifties would have appreciated the contact lenses we take for granted today.

Most singers are associated with a particular repertoire throughout their careers and Richard may have guessed that one of the works in this list would assume a special place in his life. It was music which he had heard sung by the celebrated tenor, Heddle Nash, and there was much in those performances which he admired. *The Dream of Gerontius*, Elgar's masterpiece for mezzo-soprano,

---

* Sir John Tooley succeeded Sir David Webster as General Administrator of the Royal Opera House.

tenor, baritone, choir and orchestra, is a much loved work which the composer himself regarded as containing his most inspired writing. To hear it is to take part in a religious experience. To sing it may not require religious conviction, but when the part of Gerontius is sung by a man with beliefs as firmly held as Richard's, the result is an experience, not merely a performance. Sir John Tooley recalls Heddle Nash's response to a compliment after he had just sung *Gerontius*: 'The notes were in the right place,' he said, with a no-nonsense shrug of his shoulders. Elgar said of the part 'I've not filled his part with church tunes and rubbish, but a good, healthy, full-blooded, romantic, remembered, worldliness, so to speak.' Nevertheless, *Gerontius* is profoundly devotional, and the setting of Newman's poem touches us all, Catholics or otherwise. Richard was of course a Methodist, and Newman's words may have had a distinctly foreign feel, but to hear him is to believe.

Richard would never forget that first *Gerontius* with Sargent in Liverpool for it marked the beginning of a line of performances extending thirty years into the future. It wasn't his best performance of the work; how could it be? Every interpretation must go through a process of maturation and this is particularly the case with a religious work such as *Gerontius*. Richard had his own maturing to do and many consider he attained the pinnacle when he recorded the work with Sargent. This was in 1955 when Richard was forty-one. His colleagues were Marjorie Thomas, a matchless Angel, and John Cameron. However, as many people regard Richard's second recording with Janet Baker and Kim Borg under Barbirolli as finer still. This recording dates from 1964, and if his voice has lost some freshness, this is more than compensated for by the greater humanity in the singing. A greater world-weariness describes it better.

With Barbirolli on the rostrum the overall tempo of the piece is slower; the mood more expansive. An example is the 'Sanctus Fortis' which with Sargent takes five minutes eighteen seconds. Barbirolli may take only thirteen seconds more, but those few seconds make a difference. The location could also have played a part, for Richard was on his home ground in Manchester's Free

Trade Hall. Borg was not so happy; a thick peasoup fog had him complaining that no one could sing in such weather.

Mention has been made of Richard's earnestness, but he also had a delightful sense of humour which emerged childlike and quite unexpectedly. Once, when the break was called in a rehearsal of *Gerontius*, Richard left the stage with some of the brass. Knowing these musicians would be going for a quick pint Richard quipped 'Use well the interval!', quoting directly from Newman. Never a pub man himself, he could share in their pleasure on this occasion. Others at other times would speak differently. And so on that February night in Liverpool he picked up the mantle of Gerontius and it would remain with him. It had been nobly worn by Gervase Elwes, the first Gerontius, and passed to the much admired Heddle Nash. For more than thirty years the name of Richard Lewis would be synonymous with the rôle.

For Mary Lewis the news that she was pregnant was almost too good to be true. It was eight years since their wedding and they were both in their thirties. High time for a family, friends commented when they paid a visit to Manchester in 1951.

It was not so much that they had planned it that way – for the first couple of years the war was still on and a baby would have made life even more difficult – later, Mary wanted a child, but Richard was just starting to make a name for himself. Now the timing was perfect and the new house in Pinner was ideal. It is said that nothing changes a woman more than motherhood. Becoming a father may make an enormous difference to a man, but this is not always the case. When Richard knew that a baby was on the way he was delighted and they celebrated with friends, but he did not change. Some men become more responsible, but Richard was already extremely responsible. He did not buy silly toys for the unborn child as so many prospective fathers do, or make plans to share in the baby's changing or feeding as some of today's fathers do. He did think about a name for the baby (presuming it was a boy) and decided Michael would do very well. Nothing very Welsh about that; one might have expected David or Gareth; obviously not Thomas.

A pattern of work was developing centred around Covent Garden and Glyndebourne, and the early fifties saw Richard at Glyndebourne as Ferrando in *Così fan Tutte*; the title rôle in *Idomeneo*; Admète in *Alceste*; Bacchus in *Ariadne auf Naxos*, and Tom Rakewell in *The Rake's Progress*. Meanwhile, the Royal Opera House mounted *La Traviata* and *The Fairy Queen*.

London had built the Royal Festival Hall to celebrate the Festival of Britain in 1951 and this was another concert venue where Richard appeared regularly, the Royal Albert Hall becoming a second home, with Proms appearances and *Gerontius* and the *Messiah* providing a fair contribution to his income. Always happy to travel, Richard kept his links with Europe, singing frequently in Belgium, France, Italy, and the Netherlands, and was constantly travelling in Britain, the latter being made a little easier with the introduction of lunches on the trains. He noted the six shilling menu with relish.

It was fortunate that he had little or no trouble in learning new works and his repertoire grew rapidly in these few years. Notable additions included Mahler's *Song of the Earth*, Verdi's *Requiem*, Berlioz' *Nuits d'Eté*, Kodály's *Psalmus Hungaricus*, Britten's *Spring Symphony* and, soon to be a constant companion, Beethoven's *Choral Symphony*.

But to return to Richard as a father. Although Mary felt that her husband was leaving most of the parenting to her, she accepted the situation. Richard had to concentrate on his career if he was to succeed and, if his work took him away so frequently and left him unwilling to have anything intervene, she understood and did not complain. By this time she knew that she was married to a complex man whose moods were hard to predict, and she believed the best thing she could do was to manage things at home and protect him from any unnecessary disturbances. Fortunately, as she was a musician herself, his changing moods were more easily understood and the good ones made up for the bad. Michael duly arrived on the night of the 23/24 March 1952 and Richard, just in from Amsterdam, visited the hospital in the morning and afternoon.

He was constantly on the go and his schedule would have been impossible for most people. Blessed with a seemingly inexhaustible supply of energy he took on everything he was offered and thought nothing of it. Glyndebourne provided the opera for the Edinburgh Festival in the early fifties and the range of work with which Richard was involved is testament to his versatility.

Every artist needs to relax, and to escape to Lords or the Oval was his greatest delight. Perhaps he imagined himself taking guard, who knows? His diary provides no evidence to concern an anxious wife, only mention of a few precious hours alone at a test match or important county fixture. Cricket, like chess, is a game for analysts, and Richard derived enormous pleasure from the drama it contains. Anyone who shares this enthusiasm will readily understand.

Another passion was driving, and his interest in cars was no less than that: a passion. He bought several fine cars between 1946 and 1956, and drove very well if rather too fast. The day he brought home his favourite Mercedes-Benz, it crossed Mary's mind that he was moving into the fast lane. She was sure it meant trouble.

1953 saw Richard as Tom Rakewell in Stravinsky's *The Rake's Progress,* and the beginning of an important association with the composer. In fact Stravinsky was so pleased with Richard's performance that when his *Sacrum Canticum* was premièred a few years later he insisted Richard should sing the tenor solo. Many would say that this Rakewell was the finest they had seen. No problem in getting inside a character so different from his own, Richard's acting was appreciated almost as much as his singing of the part, although it is the voice that distinguished clarinettist Jack Brymer recalls. Even from the pit of Edinburgh's King's Theatre, where the Royal Philharmonic spent the season, he was impressed with what he heard. 'Of all the singers at Glyndebourne, Richard was the musician I recall the most. He had a wonderful line in his singing and everything he did was highly intelligent.' Rare praise from one of the greatest orchestral players and wind soloists of the time, a section of the musical fraternity not easily impressed. He goes on, 'Richard took himself very seriously indeed, but even he was amused on one occasion when the bread machine refused to be cranked in the usual direction. Mind you, the amusement was mixed with irritation that someone had placed the machine the wrong way round. Richard liked people to get things right! Of course I'd heard him at the start of his career and watched him develop.' Those visits to the cinema in Manchester had not been solely to while away an hour or two, and Brymer had spotted something in Richard's style – 'I thought Richard Tauber's influence showed strongly,' he says.

In terms of development, the reviews of Richard's operatic work during the years 1947-1951 are fascinating. Even when allowance is made for the opinions of different individuals on different occasions, the progress of the young tenor is evident.

Glyndebourne Season 1947 *The Times*
The Rape of Lucretia (Male Chorus), Benjamin Britten
'Of the new singers Mr Richard Lewis may be commended for his delivery of the elaborate declamation assigned to the Male Chorus.'

Glyndebourne in Oxford 1947 R. B-S *The Oxford Mail*
'Britten relies on the Chorus (particularly well sung on the male side by Richard Lewis) to paint the scene.'

English Opera Group 1948 *Birmingham Mail*
Albert Herring (Albert), Benjamin Britten
'Richard Lewis, who played the name part, is a comedy actor of great talent as well as a first rate tenor.'

Glyndebourne at the Bath Festival 1948
F.M. Lyne *Evening World*
Il Seraglio (Belmonte), Mozart
'Richard Lewis, as Belmonte, sang his impassioned lyrics with an exquisiteness of voice rare in operatic tenors.'

Covent Garden in Birmingham 1949
J.F.W. *Birmingham Post*
Peter Grimes (Peter), Benjamin Britten
'As the gossip-haunted fisherman, Richard Lewis brings lovely singing to the lyrical and introspective passages, and makes a most moving thing of the final despairing monologue...'

Covent Garden in Liverpool 1949
Ronald Settle *Liverpool Evening Express*
'In addition to his fine singing, Mr Lewis has an acting tech-
nique that made his Peter Grimes a very real character.'

Covent Garden in Edinburgh 1950 *The Scotsman*
'The first act took a little time to warm up, but the second and
third grew in horrifying tension. This was largely due to Richard
Lewis who gave one of his best performances. Two details stick
in the mind – his expression in Act II when he heard the baying
of the pursuing villagers, and his fragments of song in the last
scene.'

Royal Opera House Covent Garden 1951 *The Telegraph*
The Magic Flute (Tamino), Mozart
'Richard Lewis, who recently sang in Dublin, is the finest
Tamino heard here since the war. He is a born Mozart
singer, combining accuracy with apparent ease.'

It goes without saying that there were less favourable notices
than these, but they are few and far between and never to do with
the voice, which is always admired. Where Richard had some work
to do was in the area of his Italian pronunciation, and about this he
was well aware. His lessons in the language slowly brought about
an improvement and he continued to perfect his accent whenever
possible throughout his career, but he was never entirely happy
with his efforts in this direction.

In every musical performer's life there is a group of works with
which they are associated, and Richard was no exception. Of his
operatic rôles, unquestionably Tom Rakewell in *The Rake's
Progress* is one, and it came to him early. Richard had been singing
with Glyndebourne opera for only six years by this time, but was
used to the King's Theatre, where the company appeared as part of
the Edinburgh Festival. The production was spectacular, by all
accounts, and between them Carl Ebert and Osbert Lancaster, who
was responsible for the designs, gave Britain the most important
operatic event of the year.

The story of a young man's riotous living is based on Hogarth's

famous series of drawings of a fall from grace and the libretto by
W. H. Auden and Chester Kallman contains many elements both
grim and happy. The authors are responsible for the character Nick
Shadow, who is the Devil in disguise, and whose malevolent
influence is central to the opera. Stravinsky's score is as always
remarkable and the work is as captivating as it is demanding.
Originally the part of Tom Rakewell was to be sung by David Lloyd,
the American tenor; however he was taken ill and replaced by
Richard, who took over with the shortest of notice and learnt the
part in three days lying on a beach in the south of France. The cast
included Nan Merriman, Elsie Morison and Jerome Hines; consequently Richard was in good company. The personality of Tom
demanded great acting from a man so completely at odds with the
character, and the music is notoriously difficult. Some said it would
be too demanding for an artist with only six years' experience, but
Richard had no doubts. He had been waiting twenty years for an
opportunity like this, and the score held no terrors for him.

The first performance at the Edinburgh Festival took place on
25th August 1953. It was conducted by Alfred Wallenstein and the
next day's papers were unanimous. The production was a great
success and Richard Lewis was a star.

For Cecil Smith of the *Scottish Daily Express* it was a night to
remember. After a detailed analysis of the performance he wrote:

'As Tom Rakewell, Richard Lewis gave the performance of his
career. His apt handling of the fearfully difficult music and his
sensitive acting showed him to be one of the few truly stellar
British opera singers.'

The Times music critic had this to say:

'Mr Richard Lewis as Tom Rakewell gave further proof of the
extraordinary versatility that he now commands – he is increasingly at home on the stage and the use of his voice has acquired
many subtleties of dramatic expression.'

Richard Capell in the *Daily Telegraph* was equally positive:

'Richard Lewis shouldered the responsibilities of the part of
the Rake with an authority and vocal quality which heartened

his admirers. The part is ungrateful in the second act, but in the first and third Mr Lewis more than fulfilled our expectations. This was one of the outstanding performances of what is clearly going to be a most distinguished career.'

Richard relished the part. It challenged the musician in him as well as the singer. More, it required acting of the greatest subtlety and he knew now, at last, that he had the stage technique required. What a happy coincidence that the character's name was Tom. Perhaps the holiday in Paris just two weeks before opening, where he and Mary had celebrated their tenth wedding anniversary, had supplied the necessary zing.

While 1953 and *The Rake's Progress* established Richard as a new operatic star, a year later he would have a chance which few singers are given: to create a rôle. As with so many events in his life, the timing appears to have been calculated to perfection.

Just as Richard was leaving the army to begin his career in London, Sir William Walton was approached by the BBC for an opera intended to be broadcast. Walton was a notoriously slow worker and the original concept for *Troilus and Cressida* grew larger during its composition (which spanned seven years) until it ended up as a grand opera unparalleled in British music.

Sir John Tooley, a later General Administrator of the Royal Opera House, recalls with amusement Walton's procrastination. 'He had to find a particular pencil. Then his rubber was missing. Everything had to be just so before he could start. Then he would work with complete concentration for several hours and manage to complete one bar!' The effort involved over this long period was enormous for a man of fifty who was attempting his first opera. The text was by Christopher Hassall, who took his inspiration from Chaucer rather than Shakespeare and provided Walton with some firmly drawn characters; but there was a problem in relation to the opera's structure and Walter Legge, founder of the Philharmonia Orchestra, advised Walton to return to the drawing board and delay the first performance. For better or worse, Walton was not prepared to listen and the production went ahead. No doubt the intense labour of composition was a factor in Walton's reluctance to postpone, but there was also the question of *Peter Grimes*. Benjamin Britten's opera had been hailed as a masterpiece and was firmly established in the repertoire of several important houses. For Walton, there was the not unreasonable desire to launch his answer, and in any case he thought that Legge was making too much of the structure problem. So far as Richard was concerned the chance came just at the right moment, when he and his voice were ready for it.

The part of Troilus is heroic and requires a tenor of heroic voice and looks. Not for the first time, Richard was compared with the film star, Stewart Granger, and the ardent, soaring lines of Walton's music were tailor-made for the virile tenor. In Spain and Italy it is often said that bull fighters and tenors aim their best passes and highest notes from the most vulnerable part of a man's anatomy and there is no doubting Richard's masculine courage as he calls for his Cressida.

A splendid cast included Magda Laszlo as Cressida, Peter Pears (in an outstanding performance) as Pondarus, and smaller parts sung by Geraint Evans and Monica Sinclair. Sir Malcolm Sargent was in charge of the musical direction. The reviews confirmed Walter Legge's concern for structure, but were warm in praise of an addition to the repertoire that was likely to prove popular. Cecil Smith summed up this view: 'It is an opera everyone can understand and enjoy. It will advance the love of opera at home and enhance the fame of Britain abroad.' Noël Goodwin was in agreement: *Troilus and Cressida* thoroughly deserved the enthusiastic reception it received at its first performance. It is grand opera in the truest sense and one which, I am sure, will add much both to Walton's stature as a composer and to the prestige of British opera.'

There was universal admiration for Richard. Without exception the critics were pleased. Percy Cater in the *Daily Mail* expressed it very simply: 'Richard Lewis as Troilus sang superbly. There is no other word for it.'

It was during this period that Richard heard some words of praise which both humbled and thrilled him following two performances of *Gerontius*. The first comment came from Sir Malcolm Sargent following their concert in Liverpool on the 13th March 1954: 'I haven't heard *Gerontius* sung so movingly since the days of Gervase Elwes,' he told him. It must have been a month for *Gerontius*, as the organist and conductor Dr Arnold Grier took Richard on one side after a performance in the Royal Albert Hall and told him he had played many times when Elwes was singing, but never had he heard the equal of that evening. 'It is the finest I ever heard,' he said simply. Marjorie Thomas was grateful to Richard, not only for the inspiration of his singing, but the advice he gave to her at a rehearsal in Liverpool. Taking her on one side, he urged her not to look at the score when the Angel responded to Gerontius' questions. 'It must be spontaneous,' he told her. Marjorie did her homework and sang it from memory thereafter. 'He was absolutely right,' she says.

When British actors became star performers, an invitation to Hollywood sometimes followed. Could something similar happen to a British opera singer?

In 1955 *Troilus and Cressida* went on tour and the provinces were equally enthusiastic as they witnessed increasingly polished performances. Glasgow's was the first presentation outside London.

Covent Garden in Glasgow 1955 M.L. *Glasgow Bulletin*
Troilus and Cressida, Sir William Walton
'Power is what this score so abundantly possesses, and what the great theme demands. What a relief, incidentally, to find for a change a major British opera of heroic proportions which doesn't hover lovingly over refinements of cruelty. Power of singing and playing is what Richard Lewis so abundantly fills out the part of Troilus with. His was a performance worthy of the leading dramatic tenor of our time.'

For Richard it came as no surprise when he was invited to sing the rôle in Los Angeles and San Francisco and so became the first British singer to be engaged by a major American opera company since Eva Turner in Chicago before the war. With these performances Richard's international career was firmly launched and the door opened for other fine artists, such as Geraint Evans to follow.

In his autobiography *A Knight at the Opera*, the great bass-baritone writes of his invitation to sing the Music Master in *Ariadne auf Naxos* at San Francisco in 1959. 'Richard Lewis travelled on the same flight with me. He had been there before, having sung the first American production of Walton's *Troilus and Cressida*.'

When, on a later occasion Richard was in San Francisco with Geraint and Michael Langdon for performances of Alban Berg's *Wozzeck*, Leopold Ludwig told them 'that it was a special pleasure to work with British singers, because they were always thoroughly prepared and could therefore be more responsive to the style of production and performance.' Evans had been much taken by Richard's singing long before they met when he was looking for a recording of Britten's *Serenade*. He was working for the British Forces Network radio station in Hamburg at the end of the war. 'I was presenting a programme of recordings which included Britten's *Serenade for Tenor, Horn and Strings* and had to choose between two available recordings, one with Peter Pears, the other with Richard Lewis. I preferred the latter, not knowing either singer at the time, and so became an admirer of Richard's vocal qualities even before I met him.'

We cannot leave this period in Richard's career without recalling his work in three more operas from the Glyndebourne repertoire: Mozart's *Idomeneo*, when he had the title rôle; Gluck's *Alceste*, in which he sang Admète; and Strauss' *Ariadne auf Naxos*, in the rôle of Bacchus.

With every appearance he underlined his position as the leading operatic tenor in the country and what had been achieved in oratorio (and continued to be, for his concert engagements at home and abroad were dovetailed between his theatrical appearances) was now established in the opera house. The critics had approved him from the start; now they lauded him:

Glyndebourne at the King's Theatre, Edinburgh, 1953
Idomeneo Mozart. G.C.M. *Glasgow Herald* 3.9.53
'Richard Lewis is a singer who has built for himself an enviable reputation. it is only possible to say that his *Idomeneo* is another achievement. His singing of the final blessing to the king was on the highest level.'

Glyndebourne at the Edinburgh Festival, 1954
Ariadne auf Naxos (Bacchus)
A.K. Holland, *Liverpool Daily Post* 26.8.54
'Richard Lewis, classified in this cosmopolitan gallery as English, was a most impressive Bacchus and his stature has never seemed so great or his singing more impressive than in the final duet.'

Glyndebourne at home in Sussex, 1954
Alceste (Admète) *The Times* 25.6.54
'Mr Richard Lewis, who stresses the humanity more than the kingliness of Admetus, was again in superlative voice, and left no doubt whatsoever that England need never search overseas for its operatic tenors.'

Like Italy, Wales is a country of singers, but unlike Italy, there have been few Welsh composers; consequently its contribution to music has been more reproductive than creative.

With his opera, *Menna*, Arwel Hughes composed a theatrical work which was enthusiastically received and his collaboration with the scholar, Wyn Griffiths, boded well for Welsh music. The Welsh National Opera Company staged the opera following earlier broadcasts and Richard sang Gwyn opposite the Menna of Elsie Morison. The simple story (for once, an opera is let down by too little incident) has not helped the work to find performances since then, but Richard was always proud to have been associated with that first production in 1953.

It is frequently said that in the world of opera the possessor of a fine lyric tenor voice can write his own cheque. The costs of opera production are huge and the employment of expensive voices from abroad adds significantly to the bill. Richard was therefore in an enviable position and Covent Garden gave him many opportunities to show what he could do. Strangely, he was not entirely happy with his own performances in Puccini and Verdi, although most critics appreciated his great musical qualities. Having heard Gigli before the war and Bergonzi, Di Stefano and Corelli more recently, Richard believed that Italian opera was best left to the Italians.

Nevertheless Richard brought to this repertoire an unusual sensitivity and musicianship as well as the top notes required. David Webster was the general administrator at the Royal Opera House and cast Richard most successfully as Alfredo in *La Traviata* with the lovely Spanish soprano Pilar Lorengar. Jess Walters sang his father.

Webster was a distinguished director and largely responsible for Covent Garden's development after the war; however, he was a restrained man and this affected his relationship with certain artists, including Richard, who felt he could have been more supportive. He complained that Webster was rarely to be seen backstage following a performance, when encouragement from the management was most needed. Sir John Tooley, who succeeded Webster, believes Richard misunderstood: 'David was not the extrovert impresario often to be found in charge of an opera house. He was extremely shy, and very concerned not to say the wrong thing immediately after the curtain came down. It was his policy to wait a few days until excitable temperaments had cooled and speak to the artists then.' Richard viewed things differently, and it angered him not a little.

In January 1955 stage rehearsals began for Tippett's *The Midsummer Marriage* and Richard found himself partnering Joan Sutherland. The other couple in the opera were Adèle Leigh and John Lanigan. Tippett's music was praised by Philip Hope-Wallace in the Manchester *Guardian*: 'The music, if not well organised (any more than the drama), turns out to be warm-blooded, generous, and often of the greatest beauty,' he wrote, following the first performance on the 27th January. The soloists were all in good voice and the opera was generally well received in spite of living up to the anticipation of those who said it would be bewildering.

It was Adèle Leigh's first meeting with Richard and she recalls the long rehearsal period well. 'He had a tough barrier in place and nothing one did could alter that. He came round in his own good time and once the barrier was down he could be very funny! I've never known a more dedicated singer, or one who took his work and himself more seriously. Richard loved the Garden, but he loved Glyndebourne even more. For him it was home, make no mistake.

I regret not having sung there myself. In fact Moran Caplat asked me to sing in *The Rake's Progress*, but I was offered an engagement in Rhodesia at the same time and since I could never resist the chance to travel I turned him down. He never asked me again!'

Adèle was very impressed with Richard's attention to the words. 'I learned a great deal from him. I'll never forget standing in the wings listening to his big aria in *The Midsummer Marriage*. It was a splendid performance of the most difficult music and I congratulated him when he came off. "Well, I did my best," he said simply. That summed up his attitude to things.'

Working with Joan Sutherland was an exhilarating experience and Richard recognised as he did with Luciano Pavarotti when they sang together at Glyndebourne, that he was hearing a voice of exceptional promise: no less than a future world star.

Dame Joan looks back forty years to her collaboration with Richard and in her own down-to-earth no-nonsense way speaks of his professionalism and outstanding musicianship in two collaborations. One she remembers particularly well, as it was her first engagement with Richard following the birth of her son Adam, and the range of the soprano part in *La Clemenza di Tito* was very demanding after her confinement. 'Richard had flown in from America and had joined us for this BBC production of Mozart's opera. We were at that stage in the first rehearsal when we needed all the help we could get, but Richard was amazing in the speed with which he learned everything. I recall he wanted to know precise points of interpretation straight away. "Should it be like this, or like that?" he demanded. He was extremely musical and highly intelligent. Like the rest of us, he wanted to get on with the job and hurry home afterwards.'

Another occasion was *The Midsummer Marriage*. 'I remember I asked Michael Tippett a question about the plot, which I found confusing. "Don't worry, darling, just sing everything beautifully and the rest will take care of itself," he said. Mozart or Tippett, it made no difference to Richard, who mastered the most difficult music in the shortest possible time. His shyness was never a problem so far as I was concerned.' One amusing aspect of *The Midsummer Marriage* Dame Joan recalls was the variety of accents in the cast.

'My Australian, Adèle's half-Canadian, Otakar's [Krauss] Czech.' Presumably there was no problem in understanding Richard. Distinguished critic Felix Aprahamian appreciated the opera very much, and the fascinating psychology of Tippett's own libretto. He bitterly regrets there is no recording with Joan Sutherland and Richard who sang so wonderfully.

Dame Joan's view of Richard's reserve is interesting. Perhaps Richard responded more easily to people who didn't try to get to know him. Exercising control in the way that he did meant that he needed to be in charge of the events in his life. To give in to the efforts of others to establish a relationship would require that he allowed that control to pass to another. That was something he never entirely learned to do. Richard was never a man to go with the flow in social terms. On the other hand, musically, few flowed more easily.

At home, Mary was enjoying those first years with Michael and was sad that Richard was away so much and unable to spend more time with them. If only he could divide things up better, she thought; but the career was gathering momentum and there seemed to be no way of slowing it down without the risk of losing the next big opportunity.

Finally a break came and they went on holiday to Bournemouth. It did them all good and Richard bought some toys for Michael and played at being a father, but even that week was broken with a return to London for a rehearsal. Still, it was a special rehearsal with the great Bruno Walter of the Mozart *Requiem* and that was not to be missed, however important the reason. An international career was in the offing and sacrifices would have to be made.

Voyage Round the World

On 25th August 1955, Richard left Southampton on board the *Queen Elizabeth* and began a love affair with the United States which would last the rest of his career. He was due to spend five weeks in San Francisco, two weeks in Los Angeles, and to sing in three performances in San Diego, Pasadena and Sacramento. Whatever excitement he had felt in the past – for instance on the occasion of his debut at Covent Garden – paled by comparison, for he saw himself as an advance guard for the other British singers who would surely follow – provided of course that he fulfilled the expectations of his American hosts. He thought back to the moment when the huge vessel cast off and his throat tightened painfully as he recalled Mary and Michael, his mother and Vera, waving good-bye.

His cabin was quite luxurious and he received what we should call VIP treatment today. He had been told the food would be good, but good was no way to describe what he was offered. 'It was wonderful,' he said. For Richard food was always important. He loved to tuck into the dishes he enjoyed and the steaks served on the great liner were unlike anything he'd seen in England, even in the excellent London restaurants he frequented. The shell fish, another irresistible food, were the largest and most succulent he had ever seen. Even the rice pudding, which he believed no-one could prepare as his mother did, was magnificent. It was all a dream come true. He spent hours on the deck sunning himself and thinking how far he had come since those miserable days at the CPA. Was that really him? Surely not. Someone he used to know. Tom Thomas, not Richard Lewis. He turned his thoughts back to Mary and Michael and went in search of the telegraphist to book a call for the following evening. He would be a thousand miles out to sea when they put him through to Pinner. It was an odd idea telephoning on the move. Not being at a fixed point. Not even on land.

They had been married for twelve years. It seemed barely possible; the time had sped by. Michael was three now and a fine boy, but he barely knew him. He needed to put that right. Mary was proud of his success, and his father would have been too, if only he could have lived a while longer to see. The success he had longed for was finally his. At least his mother was still with them. His name was known to everyone in British music, and to many in countries like Holland and Austria. Now he was to sing in America and his reputation as an international artist would be sealed. That was the way the press was writing. Britain's first international tenor. Others even extended it to singer.

Would they like him in San Francisco and Los Angeles? He pondered the question. Would they like *Troilus and Cressida*? Strange to be singing to an English-speaking audience in a country so far away, so different, so foreign. In a way, more foreign than Holland or Austria could ever be.

Five days later the *Queen Elizabeth* arrived in New York and docked at Pier 90. For the next two months Richard was taken under the wings of his hosts and treated like visiting royalty. The food of the liner continued on land and he was overwhelmed with the generosity of everyone he met. So many new impressions crowded together in a dazzling panorama which pleased and fatigued him in equal measure. It was so important to be in good form for his performances and he tried to combine the entertaining and sight-seeing with the professional demands, but this was difficult. He looked at his reflection in the mirror and saw where some of the hospitality had gone.

The importance of that first visit to America cannot be overestimated, not only because Richard was making his reputation in the country where it mattered most, but he was also experiencing the joy of being among people with whom he could be at ease with himself. For Richard, it was like a breath of fresh air. He was enthusiastically received by opera lovers as a star of the Royal Opera House, and for the media, he was a star from Europe with a difference, in that he could be interviewed on the radio, and by the press, with no language problems. His contacts had no interest in, or understanding of, British class divisions, and Richard's polite but direct approach was similar to American behaviour. In Britain Richard had moved easily enough into the ranks of the middle class and was freely accepted by everyone he met, but, unfortunately, he could not forget his background and he still harboured some social misgivings. In New York, San Francisco and Los Angeles, he was simply Richard Lewis, the celebrated tenor, and, since he behaved like a gentleman, he *was* a gentleman.

Those first days in New York were enthralling. He couldn't get over the skyline. Several times he bumped into people in the street as he walked with head thrown back looking to the top of sky-scrapers first seen in the cinema. The RCA, the Woolworth, and of course the Empire State Building. People moved more quickly here and were intent upon getting to their destinations. The pulse of life was faster and he couldn't help but feel excited by it. He, Richard Lewis, the Welsh tenor from Manchester, was about to show them what he could do.

Apart from *Troilus and Cressida*, Richard was appearing with the San Francisco Opera in *Butterfly* and *Carmen*. The demands on his voice were considerable, but the rôles of Don José, Pinkerton and Troilus are similarly romantic and the switch from one to another is not extreme in terms of mood and expression. Richard wished to pace himself through the heavy rehearsal schedule and frequent performances – he sang two or three times a week – and still see as much of the country as he could. He was entertained by the Wallensteins, and Virginia made it her business to see that he was introduced to as many of the musical establishment as she could. Wishing to complete his American education she saw to it that he went to a football match and, when the Company appeared in Los Angeles, that visits to Hollywood included Warner Brothers

Studios, where he met Mario Lanza and the film composer Johnny Green – and enjoyed the best food California could provide.

2nd November was a red letter day in Richard's diary, when he had lunch at Stravinsky's North Wetherley Drive home and they discussed Richard's interpretation of Tom Rakewell. Stravinsky was the chef and served a delicious spaghetti, appropriately dressed and complete with an apron.

Most of the reviews were favourable towards the productions and praised Richard for his singing and acting. Kurt Herbert Adler, the director of the San Francisco Opera was delighted by his new find, and the New York agent Siegfried Hearst of NCAC was eager to sign him to an exclusive contract, as were Columbia Artists. No doubt they had read Alfred Frankenstein's review of *Carmen* which ended: 'Lewis's Don José is one of the greatest interpretations of the part I have yet heard.' A rare tribute from America's leading opera critic.

Richard's last performance of the tour was as Don José, in Fresno, and he left New York on BOAC at 5pm on 13th November. He was due to sing *Gerontius* in Leeds just three days later and discovered, to his delight, that he was not unduly affected by the rapid change of time. With the new career that this first US trip initiated, this was a welcome discovery.

The year had started on a sad note with the memorial service at St. Sepulchre's, Holborn, for the much-loved contralto Gladys Ripley, who Richard believed was underestimated as a result of Kathleen Ferrier's remarkable talent. Gladys was only forty-six when she died in 1955 in Chichester and the oratorio world was robbed of a second outstanding alto voice within the space of two years. She was a wonderful Angel in Elgar's *Dream of Gerontius*, and Richard was very upset by her death.

Increasingly the need to pack as much as possible into his life gripped him, and his commitments included *The Magic Flute* at Covent Garden and *Così fan Tutte* at Glyndebourne. He visited Vienna to rehearse Mozart's *Requiem* and the *Coronation Mass* with Josef Krips in preparation for the Edinburgh Festival and recorded *Idomeneo* under Rafael Kubelik at Abbey Road and the Kingsway Hall.

One event made 1956 the most memorable year in Mary's life as a musician, and it is important to remember that although she had not touched the flute in any serious way since her student days in Manchester, she remained a keen music lover. After Michael's birth in 1952 she had limited her travel to a minimum in order to stay close to home, but in September she flew to Venice with Richard to hear him sing in the first performance of Stravinsky's *Canticum Sacrum* in St Mark's (13.9.56).

Many details of that evening remain with her and particularly the journey by gondola which Stravinsky's party made to a restaurant for supper after the performance. At eighty she no longer remembers the name of the restaurant, but her happiness in being given the place of honour next to the great composer as he entertained his guests is vividly recalled.

The *Canticum Sacrum*, like the ballet *Agon,* contains serial elements and the solo tenor part required much from the accomplished musician Richard had shown himself to be in the *The Rake's Progress*. Stravinsky was delighted with the performance, and believed the success of the première was largely due to Richard's singing. Mary and Richard returned, tired but happy, to London in the early hours in order that he could prepare for his flight to San Francisco on 16th September and spend a few precious hours with Michael. This year's US visit involved performances of *Così fan Tutte*, as well as *Butterfly*; and *Boris Godunov* in Los Angeles.

His opera engagements in the U.S. completed, Richard returned home via Canada where a series of recitals had been arranged in Montreal, Quebec and Chicoutimi. This gave him the opportunity to renew his friendship with Leopold Simoneau, the Canadian tenor, with whom he had worked at Glyndebourne. Regarded as one of the finest Mozarteans of the day, Leopold was extremely close to Richard, and they remained firm friends throughout their careers. In fact theirs was a relationship of unusual intimacy in Richard's life, and started propitiously after Leopold sang at the Aix-en-Provence Festival, and Richard recommended him to Glyndebourne. An extremely generous act on the part of a tenor of very similar type.

Perhaps to compensate for spending so much time away from

home, in 1957 Richard decided to take Mary and Michael on tour to America, Australia and New Zealand. Although he was only five, Michael appreciated being with his father more than ever before, and his only regret today is that he was not old enough to fully understand all that they did together.

They left Southampton on the Queen Mary at the beginning of May and spent a few days in New York, where Michael was taken to Central Park Zoo and saw the world-famous collection of animals, but he remembers most a ride in a pony cart. In Los Angeles they spent a day at Disneyland and Richard had made a courtesy call on Kurt Herbert Adler. Meanwhile, Mary went to the film studios and spent some time visiting Santa Barbara and Carmel with Virginia Wallenstein.

The weather was mixed, but they took themselves to the beach and Mary took full advantage of the long days with Richard in the most relaxed period she had known since they married. Fourteen years of marriage during war and peace, and now, at last, some of the good things for which they had both worked so hard. Perhaps this holiday would mark the beginning of a new relationship between Richard and Michael. She desperately hoped so.

On to Honolulu by ship and from there to New Zealand and Australia, which for Richard was the working part of the trip, including performances at Christchurch, Dunedin, Queenstown, Wellington and Auckland. The recital programmes were of his choosing, with some local requests, and the concerts included Verdi's *Requiem*, *Les Illuminations* and *Gerontius*. Sometimes Mary took Michael on ahead: to Sydney by sea, for instance, while Richard completed his engagements in New Zealand before joining them in Australia. His voice was in perfect condition and he looked much younger than his forty-three years. When he arrived in Melbourne for his Town Hall recital, he discovered a very large poster complete with a drawing bearing no resemblance to him which caused him to complain to his diary. But this blemish in publicity apart, every date was highly successful and he indulged each moment of sunshine.

Mary and Michael returned to England on 9th September and Richard continued on to Adelaide and Perth. His last concerts were in Hobart before he left for his American engagement on October 1st. He had been away from England for five months and, judging by the happiness expressed in his diary, had suffered no homesickness. Without question the story would have been very different had Mary and Michael not been with him – that was one of the reasons for taking them along – but absence from England was not a problem for Richard, and we may conclude that he was more at ease when abroad. Certainly the outdoor existence and lifestyle of Australia and California appealed enormously; and yet the conventional side of Richard's nature was pleased by those things he could more easily find in the musical world of Europe.

This year, the San Francisco season involved him in an opera by Richard Strauss, his *Ariadne auf Naxos,* and with his colleague Geraint Evans also in the cast there was certain to be a great deal of fun and games. It is hard to imagine two characters more different; nevertheless Richard and Geraint got on famously and Geraint's larger-than-life personality brought out the humour and mischief that were always present, but frequently buried beneath Richard's serious side. From almost identical backgrounds, they had the greatest respect for one another's vocal achievements, and Geraint was full of praise for Richard's unique musicianship.

Joan Ingpen was prominent in artists' management at that time and was regarded as an outstanding authority on singers. Her admiration for Richard knew no bounds and she firmly believed Britain's leading tenor should be singing at New York's Metropolitan Opera House rather than in San Francisco. From Richard's point of view, he regarded his association with the visionary Kurt Herbert Adler as extremely rewarding and the repertoire offered him as tailor-made.

Before returning to London Richard paid a visit to Vancouver for a performance of *Gerontius* and finally a hugely successful *Das Lied von der Erde* with the St. Louis Symphony Orchestra.

There was just time for dinner with the Adlers in New York and an important meeting with Herbert Barrett, President of the prominent US concert agency, before catching his flight to London on the 7th December. Within forty-eight hours of arriving home he was recording Gilbert and Sullivan's *Yeomen of the Guard*. Perhaps it was the most appropriate music with which the errant British tenor could announce his return.

Elizabeth

'Who is that?' asked a statuesque young member of the company, in what she hoped was *sotto voce*. A colleague provided the name of Glyndebourne's star tenor, no doubt amused by the emphasis on the first word of the question, which indicated the enquiry was not based on entirely musical considerations. The rehearsal continued for several minutes until someone called the break.

They were on stage for the first rehearsal of Gluck's *Alceste*, and Richard had been working hard for more than an hour. 'Has anyone got a sweet for me?' he asked, turning to the group. A blond head disappeared in the direction of the dressing rooms and returned with the badly-needed throat easer. Richard took a long look at this Good Samaritan and asked himself two things. The first, who was she, and the second, why was he feeling decidedly confused?

Aged forty-four, Richard was at the peak of his career. Established as Britain's leading tenor and secure financially, falling in love was not in his programme for 1958. His fees during the last two years had risen dramatically, and with Wilfred Stiff in London and Herbert Barrett taking care of things in America, he could relax a little and enjoy the fruits of his labours. Pinner had been very nice, but after nine years and the chance to see how others lived, Richard was yearning for something more. There was money in the bank, and he could well afford Fairfield with its tennis court and swimming pool. A pure coincidence, but a happy one, that the name of the house was linked to Manchester in countless ways.

With a bit of luck his career would last for another twenty years and then he could retire and do some teaching, or perhaps conduct. Either way Michael would be off their hands by then and they could settle down to a quiet lifestyle and enjoy all they'd worked for. But first of all he must find out her name.

It was Robertson, and it took him straight back to those difficult years at the CPA. Hilda Robertson had impressed him, too, that summer of 1937, but he had been strong and stuck to his music. Obviously the temptation had been there, but he had his sights set on other things, and the desire to be a professional singer came first.

Elizabeth was the daughter of the well-known television journalist Fyfe Robertson, and Richard quickly discovered that her personality was equally attractive to him and that his first instincts had not been wrong. In 1958 however, nicely brought up girls of twenty-three gave married men of forty-plus a wide berth and it had taken very little time for Elizabeth to confirm what she had guessed; Richard Lewis was a married man.

'Love at first sight' is a phrase inclined to produce smiles of superiority from those who have never experienced it. For Richard and Elizabeth there was never any question but that their relationship began with that shock of recognition and, what is more, stood the test of time.

And so began the torture of leading a secret life and the discreet assignations relished by many men were nothing less than torture for Richard. For Elizabeth, too, there was another kind of agonising. Not religious in any profound way, she did have a code of conduct instilled by her mother, which did not permit her to do what she was doing – judged by today's standards, not very much – but she was quite hopelessly in love.

Young though she was, Elizabeth had her own career ambitions. She had studied at the Royal College of Music and was regarded as a promising young soloist at Glyndebourne. In addition to the small trio in *Alceste* she was understudying major rôles and her vocal talent and good looks augured well for her future professional career. Her emotions were understandably in turmoil; however once the season was over there was respite in the form of a Caird scholarship which she had won to study in Vienna, and which would keep them apart for at least a year. Her parents consoled themselves that a lot could happen in a year.

That season also saw Richard as Bacchus in Strauss' *Ariadne auf Naxos*, and Marjorie Thomas, who had sung the part of Dryade in an earlier production under Beecham speaks with admiration, and not a little wonder, at the way Richard, with his lyric tenor voice, handled the expansive phrases of 'Heldentenor' writing in the famous duet with Ariadne. 'He had found a way to propel his voice that was a revelation,' she says.

At the beginning of August, Richard recorded *The Rake's Progress* for BBC Television and on the 8th there was a special occasion at Glyndebourne with the wedding of John Christie's son George to Mary Nicholson. The company was there in strength and Richard and Geraint Evans provided some of the solo entertainment. A memorable event is recorded in Richard's diary and the setting and music must have delighted the young couple and everyone attending.

A Proms date and then preparations for San Francisco limited Richard's chances to see much of Elizabeth before she left for Vienna, but they snatched a few hurried suppers and had to content themselves with these brief meetings.

Richard and Mary had been married for fifteen years by this time, and perhaps inevitably, had grown apart; for although he was a faithful husband, his frequent absences had hardly served to consolidate their relationship.

If Richard was unable to see his way ahead emotionally, one thing did help his vision, and this was the purchase of his first contact lenses in San Diego. At last he could dispense with the endless pairs of spectacles which had caused him such irritation, and, an added bonus, the cost was tax deductible!

A performance of *The Dream* with the New York Philharmonic conducted by Sir John Barbirolli, once the orchestra's music director, was undertaken with missionary zeal by tenor and conductor, who were determined to leave the Americans in no doubt that they were listening to a masterpiece.

Herbert Barrett was delighted to be representing an artist who was equally at home in the opera house, concert hall and recording studio and was enjoying unusual audience and critical acclaim. Herbert liked Richard very much and recalls how caring he was when anyone needed help. 'An emergency situation always brought out the best in Richard, and on numerous occasions he saved the day; sometimes acting as an ambulance to drive a colleague to hospital at breakneck speed, or looking after someone in distress.' Professionally, Richard was much in demand and sang with every orchestra and conductor of note. His association with Eugene Ormandy and the Philadelphia Orchestra was notable and his recording of Mendelssohn's *Elijah* with them was considered the best available.

It was this recording which Phillip Langridge heard in 1961, at the start of his singing career, which he hoped would be helpful in his own preparation of *Elijah*. 'Once I had heard Richard's recording, I couldn't get it out of my head, and I vowed that in future, I would always learn a part thoroughly and discover my own interpretation before listening to another performance on record. I soon realised that I was not Richard Lewis, and however inspirational his singing, I had to find my own way.'

Today Phillip is among the leading singers of his generation and is delighted that he has often been compared to Richard, whom he regards as something of a hero. 'He was a remarkable artist with a beautiful voice that was instantly recognisable. I recall he had a *mezza di voce* that was always available to him and which he employed quite miraculously. It would have been wonderful to have had some lessons with him, but I was much too shy to ask.' What a shame. Richard would have loved to have worked with a talent such as Phillip's.

'Richard was a great stylist who was equally at home in every era of music, and his range in oratorio and opera was unparalleled at that time.'

Phillip Langridge sang Aaron for Sir Georg Solti in Chicago in 1984, and the year before, he was Idomeneo at Glyndebourne when Richard was in the audience. 'I was thrilled when he came to see me afterwards and complimented me on my performance. It was not just his voice and musicianship which set him apart; it was his power of communication and a spiritual element in his singing which made him unique.'

Writing about Richard's recordings, the American conductor James Paul is enthusiastic about *L'incoronazione di Poppea* in which, with Hugues Cuénod, Richard sings 'the greatest drunken scene I've ever heard.' Paul hopes, too, that the superb Handel arias collection will be re-issued one day. 'Walter Süsskind once told me that Richard Lewis and Peter Pears dispelled forever the idea that tenors were stupid. For us Richard was simply one of the greats.'

Clearly, English composers were well served by Richard throughout his career, and his recordings of Gilbert and Sullivan remain unequalled by any other tenor. 'Take a Pair of Sparkling Eyes' from *The Gondoliers*, or 'A Wandering Minstrel' from *The Mikado* are two fine examples from that repertoire and an object lesson for any student. The popular broadcaster Richard Baker admired Richard, and believed his fame would have been even greater had he been singing today. Apart from the wonderful Glyndebourne performances such as *Così fan Tutte,* he singles out the English folk songs as favourites.

It was around this time that the ensemble called the Bach Aria Group came into being, and Richard's diary is dotted with BAG engagements. With colleagues such as Maureen Forrester and Lois Marshall, and outstanding instrumentalists including Oscar Shumsky, Samual Baron and Bernard Greenhouse, the group toured the United States and this chamber music work provided Richard with the perfect balance to his theatrical and large-scale concert performances. Herbert was also impressed by Richard's intellectual curiosity. 'He regretted so much his lack of formal education and was anxious that his sons should be well educated. His great hobby was photography and he was equally good with Leica and film camera, achieving quite professional results.' Evidence of this is his film on Glyndebourne which is in the British film archives. For his part, Richard was fortunate in his choice of agent, regarding Herbert Barrett and staff as the perfect management team, and Herbert as a man of great integrity.

In November, following the San Francisco Opera season and a

recording of *Das Lied von der Erde* with the Chicago Symphony, Richard was contacted urgently by Wilfred Stiff to sing the part of Mephistopheles in a concert performance of Busoni's *Dr. Faustus* at the Royal Festival Hall. The tenor engaged was indisposed and among the other soloists was Dietrich Fischer-Dieskau as Faustus. The London Philharmonic was to be conducted by Sir Adrian Boult. One remarkable aspect of this performance was that Richard began to learn the part on the plane from New York to London on 11th November, dashed to the first rehearsal at Queen Mary College, and performed it on the 13th at the Royal Festival Hall. From this point on, it was accepted internationally, that if a tenor was needed to step in at the last minute and sing an unknown work, no matter how difficult it might be, Richard Lewis was the man to get.[*]

Christmas 1959 must have been difficult for all concerned, but for Mary it was particularly hard. Her fears for the future and determination to save her marriage if it were at all possible can be understood by all of us. Her concerns for Michael, who was now seven, must have proved a constant, nagging worry. For Richard, his mind torn between Mary and Michael and their needs, and the inescapable fact of his love for Elizabeth, this was the worst period of his life. Only work could serve to distract him and he thanked God for the solace of music. However, he was less confident of his relationship with God at this time than ever before, and weighed down with a guilt which would not leave him; consequently he took on every engagement offered as a means of escape. Worry can easily destroy our best efforts with its draining demands on our minds and bodies, but in Richard's case some of his most accomplished work dates from this time and is evidence of his grit. As Herbert Barrett said 'an emergency situation brought out the best in him.'

Emergency situations at the Vienna State Opera must be the norm for visiting artists, since rehearsals are not easily arranged outside those previously scheduled. Richard asked for one when

---

[*] This concert stands out in the mind of the author who was playing in the orchestra that evening, and clearly recalls the authority of the substitute soloist in this rarely performed work

he sang *Don Giovanni* and *Die Zauberflöte* during Elizabeth's year of study, and the management agreed; however, it didn't help him in the performance, because no one thought to explain that when the curtain was lowered, the exit from the stage was unconventional, to say the least. Richard was simply asked to stand in front of the curtain for 'Dalla Sua Pace' and received a great ovation, to which he responded appropriately — but when he felt behind him for the division between the curtains, he realised with horror that there wasn't one. The fire curtain was in one piece and there was no way to reach the wings. He continued to bow and the audience continued to applaud while he searched desperately for a way off. Then he saw it. A flight of steps down into the orchestra pit provided the necessary escape. We can imagine his relief, and presumably Elizabeth's, as she sat with her friends leading the applause from the orchestra stalls. Students in Vienna never turn down the offer of a free meal, and Richard invited twenty hungry singers and musicians to supper the next evening.

Elizabeth's return from Vienna in 1962, following her studies with Erik Werba and Baron Karg, was a time for blissful reunion, although Richard was living out of a suitcase and becoming weary of hotels, and longed for a place to call his own.

His diary for 1960 is the last with his Rickmansworth address and the situation at home and start of the Glyndebourne season (*Don Giovanni* and *The Magic Flute*) obliged him to find accommodation in Sussex. A flat in Brunswick Terrace, Hove, became available and he rented it immediately. Saying goodbye to Fairfield was far from easy, for the house represented all he had worked so hard to achieve. With its tennis court and swimming pool it provided those recreations he needed away from work and to which he had first been attracted as a young man.

By now the division of his year into: spring in New York; summer in Glyndebourne; autumn in San Francisco; winter in London, was more or less established and filled out with European trips to Amsterdam, The Hague, Brussels and Vienna. His income had soared over the last few years, but the future looked ominously expensive and he knew he would need all his strength to face what lay ahead.

In America the joint recital with another artist of equal celebrity was very fashionable and Richard enjoyed these concerts enormously. The sharing of the work allowed for different programme planning, with rests between demanding arias giving time to recover from any stress to the voice; but it was a particular delight to use the collaboration to provide the audience with the greatest pleasure in terms of vocal contrast and style, and to end the recital with duets.

Among the artists Richard looked forward to working with was the charming Canadian born mezzo-soprano, Jennie Tourel. They had a great deal in common apart from their vocal styles and accomplishments and the audience loved seeing them together. Jennie was the creator (1951) of Baba the Turk in Stravinsky's *The Rake's Progress* and like Richard, she had taken another name (an anagram of her teacher's name) after studying with Anna El-Tour in Paris.

Clearly the opportunity to divide his professional activities between America, Britain and Europe suited Richard perfectly. First of all he enjoyed the travelling involved. Next he appreciated the different working conditions and the challenge this provided, and, most of all, the knowledge that his reputation was growing with every engagement. A new musical centre was added in 1961 with an invitation to sing *Das Lied von der Erde* in Israel and since even Richard could not be in two places at once, he did not sing in the San Francisco season, but accepted contrasting engagements with the Berlin and Vienna State Opera. In Berlin he sang Amphitryon in the première of *Alkmene*, and in Vienna, *Die Zauberflöte*.

Alkmene by Giselher Klebe was unusual in many ways, not least because no less than three English speaking singers appeared in it: Richard, and the Americans Thomas Stewart and Evelyn Lear. Klebe's difficult music has limited this work to infrequent performances, but praise for the guest singers was generous and the production was considered worthwhile, if testing.

Until this point, Richard could hardly have arranged better the career opportunities which came his way, but now it seemed that everyone wanted him, and all at the same time. First a contract came from the Berlin Opera, but this would have meant sacrificing many of his American engagements; and then, out of the blue, La Scala, Milan were in touch. The offer was more than tempting, but he was already committed elsewhere. He discussed the situation with Luciano Pavarotti, who was impressed with his friend's scrupulous behaviour, but pointed out that La Scala did not look kindly on singers who did not accept their invitation.

With his comprehensive musicianship and analytical mind it is not surprising to learn that Richard was fascinated by the conductor's art and felt drawn to it long before he took up the baton in later life. Today, Placido Domingo, Daniel Barenboim and Vladimir Ashkenazy are recognised as conductors while still performing as singer and pianists, but this was not usual in the sixties when Richard was in his prime.

In the main conductors liked working with Richard, because of his thorough preparation of the work in hand, but among the great conductors there was one notable exception, Dr. Otto Klemperer. Already in his seventies, Klemperer was far from being a well man, but most of his life he had been in poor health following a stroke in 1939, so there was nothing new about this. In the rehearsals for the 1962 production of *Die Zauberflöte* at Covent Garden, Richard was singing Tamino to Geraint Evans' Papageno, and they had reached a section of spoken exchange between the two characters. Not allowing them to complete the last line of the dialogue, Klemperer brought in the orchestra early. Richard asked if they could rehearse the section again. They did, but with the same early entry of the orchestra. Richard pleaded with the conductor for another run-through, pointing out what was wrong. A third attempt was made, with precisely the same result and Richard, losing his temper, did the unforgivable with stage property and hurled his flute at the backdrop. Eventually the rehearsal continued, but Klemperer was furious and determined to get his own back. In performance when Richard was singing his big aria 'Dies Bildnis' Klemperer suddenly decided to blow his nose and took some time about it, while making a clearly audible noise. Mercifully, the orchestra continued, as it was always prepared to do when Klemperer was on the box, and Richard certainly had no intention of stopping and would most probably have sung his aria through to the end – without orchestra if necessary.

Of all the conductors Richard worked with, the one he became closest to was the music director of the Philadelphia Orchestra, Eugene Ormandy. The Hungarian maestro was not an easy man and not universally popular with soloists and orchestral players, but the chemistry between him and Richard was just right. Good correspondents, they wrote frequently and arranged to get together when either was in the other's country. Musically, they saw eye to eye in the interpretation of the works they performed, and while this may seem an obvious condition for performance, it is not always easily arrived at, particularly when soloist and conductor have very different views and find compromise difficult. Recognition that a composition may be successfully performed in a variety of ways, with different tempi, dynamics and spirit, permits the interpreters to respond to one another's suggestions. It is essential that the conductor should be given the final word, but singers will be more concerned to perform in the way best suited to their vocal idiosyncrasies and breathing capacities, and less flexible than instrumental soloists. Ormandy was fifteen years older than Richard and became almost a father figure. No one could have filled the rôle better.

Another conductor with whom Richard enjoyed a warm and friendly relationship was Ormandy's compatriot Georg Solti and we can see in all three men a seriousness of purpose which led to mutual respect and understanding.

Someone who came to know Richard very well was Kay Chandler, who was appointed his dresser at Glyndebourne in 1961 and stayed with him throughout his career there. As she says, 'When you've dressed and undressed a man, and helped to apply and remove body make-up from the parts not easily reached for more than twenty years, you can be said to know him well!' Many of the confidences exchanged between the dresser and the artist in the intimacy of the dressing room at times of the greatest stress are quite clearly confidential, but some of the events she describes have been shared with others and her thoughts are her own.

The first opera for which she dressed Richard was *Fidelio,* in which he sang Florestan. Kay recalls she was advised to keep away from him because he liked to be left alone and to limit her attendance in star dressing room, No. 17, to a minimum. Richard asked her why she didn't stay in his room rather than come and go, and when she explained what she had been told he expressed surprise. 'I prefer you to stay with me,' he said, and from then on she did.

'He was a very kind man, but misunderstood by many who didn't get to know him well enough. There was a break of 1¹/2 hours between the morning and afternoon rehearsals and more than once I have seen him spend that precious rest time helping a newcomer who was having problems. I particularly remember him giving tips to Delmé Bryn-Jones when he came to do Nick Shadow, and David Hughes who was a "popular" tenor less at home in the opera house, when he sang in *Werther*.'

Sir Michael Tippett's *King Priam* is his second opera and belongs to the middle period of his composition, sometimes called the 'disjunct', to distinguish it from his first, or 'lyrical', period. In 1962 Richard sang the part of Achilles with the same success, although the demands were quite different, that he had scored in *The Midsummer Marriage* a few years earlier. The premier was at the Coventry Theatre on 29th May and it opened at Covent Garden on 5th June. Sir John Tooley remarks on Richard's 'extraordinary ability to span a phrase of the greatest length, yet finish with the most perfect *pianissimo*.' Very different dynamically, he remembers Achilles War-Cry from *King Priam* as a really thrilling and dramatic piece of singing.

That same season, the Soviet conductor Alexander Melik-Pashaev was in charge of Tchaikovsky's *Queen of Spades* in which Richard was cast as Hermann. He much appreciated the friendliness of the company, but complained that rehearsal time was far too little and contrasted the twelve days allocated, with the three or four weeks usual in Moscow.

He writes: 'Rehearsals took place in an atmosphere of mutual co-operation and so the music making was easy and pleasant. Of course, if I had had more time it would have been possible to do everything better and the principals would have had greater depth in their portrayal of rôles that were unfamiliar to them. For example,

the portrayal by the indisputably talented actor/singer Richard
Lewis had been conceived incorrectly by the producer from the
very beginning: the characterisation was superficial, not creating
the obsession that is somehow on a grand scale but replacing it
with the external features of hysteria and fussiness......'

The cast was from many nationalities: Collier (Australian),
Coates (English), Lewis (Welsh), Krauss (Czech) and Quilico
(Franco-Italian).... The dress rehearsal was on 1st December, the
first night the 2nd, with performances on the 5th, 11th, 14th and
19th, all with the same cast. Singing Hermann six times in twelve
days makes serious demands on an artist's vocal and artistic
maturity.....'*

An interesting comparison of working conditions at that time
in the Soviet Union and the West and a credit to the artists at Covent
Garden whose talent produced outstanding performances under less
than ideal conditions.

At Glyndebourne the season included Monteverdi's *L'incoronazione di Poppea* and Strauss' *Ariadne auf Naxos*. More than thirty
years later, Sir John Tooley and Kay Chandler both recall the duet
from *Poppea* which Richard sang with Magda Laszlo, as among
their favourite memories of that time. Opera director or music loving dresser, their reaction to his singing was almost identical.

Following the first performance of *King Priam* at the Coventry
Theatre 19.5.62 *The Times* critic wrote:

'Special praise must be given to the Achilles of Mr. Richard
Lewis who did full justice to two landmarks in the opera, a
song with guitar accompaniment (exquisitely played by Mr.
John Williams), and the tremendous, frenzied war-cry with
which Achilles ends the second act.'

As with so many of the leading concert artists of the time,
Richard was usually accompanied in recital by Geoffrey Parsons,
whose untimely death in January 1995 was such a great loss. An
accompanist of the greatest distinction, many looked upon him as

---

* I am indebted to Edward Morgan, Musicologist and Russian Scholar for
the translation from 'Soviet Music' 1962.

the natural successor to Gerald Moore, and Richard regarded himself as very fortunate in this association. Once, when they were in Australia, Geoffrey asked Richard to go with him to see his father who was dying. Richard agreed immediately, and even offered to sing for him. Throughout his career Richard had experienced the joy of working with a number of exceptionally gifted pianists, among them Benjamin Britten, Franz Reizenstein, Noel Mewton-Wood, John Constable and Martin Isepp.

For Martin the outstanding quality in Richard's singing was his respect for the English language. 'His diction was excellent and every word could be heard perfectly. Surtitles in the opera house are a recent and valuable aid to the audience's understanding; however they would have been almost superfluous in Richard's case, he feels. Martin played for Richard in England and the United States and recalls his musicianship with pleasure; however one recital ended on a surprise note. 'As an encore Richard sang Oliver Cromwell's Song, and when he came to the last line "if you want any more you can sing it yourself", he disappeared off stage, leaving me sitting rather foolishly at the piano. I had been given no warning of his intention and as the audience applauded enthusiastically I decided to accept their appreciation and bowed as a soloist might. I was not impressed, but I consider I got the last laugh!'

If Martin found the barrier of Richard's reserve hard to cross, as true professionals their musical collaboration came first, and any personal differences were kept under wraps. A successful recital must satisfy on several levels and appeal to an audience of different age and taste. A typical Richard Lewis recital with piano might be programmed as follows:

A Handel aria such as 'Waft Her Angels' from *Jephtha*. Then some early English songs by John Dowland. Every recital contained at least two Mozart arias. Richard often chose 'To my Beloved' from *Don Giovanni*. The programme might well end with a group of Duparc songs to which he brought an ecstatic quality of intentness which was memorable.

On the other hand, a recital with orchestra provided an opportunity for his full range: again starting with Handel and the grand delivery of 'Sound an Alarm', but including the 'Flower Song' from *Carmen* or a Puccini aria from *Tosca* or *La Bohème*. Perhaps the lovely Serenade from *The Fair Maid of Perth* by Bizet, which was such a favourite of Heddle Nash. These highlights from the tenor repertoire would be linked to less popular songs which Richard was anxious to introduce in countries with less music on offer.

Occasionally, the choice of programme would be left to the concert committee, with some surprising results. Once, in Wales, when he was singing with colleagues, Richard noticed the duets and quartets were the same as in a concert presented the year before. He was curious and asked the committee chairman why this was. The man replied promptly, 'Oh, we just wanted to see if you could sing them any better!' So much for the Welsh competitive spirit. Richard would have appreciated that.

In San Francisco Richard was booked to sing the Drum Major in Alban Berg's *Wozzeck* and Tom Rakewell in Stravinsky's *The Rake's Progress*, and it may have crossed his mind that he was becoming too closely identified with twentieth century music. In fact *La Bohème* and *Don Giovanni* were also in that season's repertoire, but Richard knew that it would be the Berg and Stravinsky the public remembered.

At forty-nine, Richard came to a crossroads in his life, and 1963 was marked by three events of the greatest importance. The first was the increasing frailty of his mother and her death on 6th May, a few days after her eighty-second birthday. The second was his marriage to Elizabeth after five years of waiting: the twenty-two years' difference were still there, but Elizabeth had matured and the love hadn't changed. The third, a well-deserved and popular honour with his decoration by Queen Elizabeth II as a Commander of the British Empire. Everyone was delighted and no one was surprised, but he was the sole musician in the New Year's Honours list. A comparable achievement in the nineties would almost certainly have brought, or been followed by, a knighthood. Vera and Michael accompanied Richard to Buckingham Palace for the investiture and he was inevitably reminded of that occasion twenty-five years before, when he attended St. James' Palace to receive his Gold Medal from the Duke of Kent. Happy and fulfilled as he was, there was no element of surprise that he had come so far. He wrote not with arrogance but with simple acceptance of his talent and unwavering faith in the source of that talent. There was no place for luck in the equation; well .. perhaps just the tiniest bit; rather it was determination based on faith.

Without father or mother, Richard felt that momentary panic which comes to us all when we are no longer anyone's child, and the remaining members of his family – sister Vera, brother-in-law David, and niece Gwyneth – assumed an even greater importance in his life.

Not many men go to work on their wedding day, but Richard did. On Saturday, 25th May 1963, Elizabeth and Richard made their vows at Brighton Methodist Church. The bride looked beauti-ful, the groom handsome, albeit mature. No one could doubt they were in love. The wedding ceremony was at two p.m. A reception followed at Shelley's Hotel in Lewes, to which most of Glynde-bourne Opera were invited and proceeded to oil voices in prepara-tion for the performance of *Fidelio* at five-forty-five. Fortunately, Lewes and Glyndebourne are no more than a stone's throw apart, but the happy occasion had an unexpected result that evening. As Kay Chandler recalls: 'The Male Chorus, who should look ill and dejected, were rosy cheeked and bushy tailed, and quite obviously the champagne reception had done the trick. Never did a chorus of prisoners look so optimistic!' Richard was in fine form as Florestan, it appears. Disciplined as ever, he had allowed himself two glasses and two glasses it was.

John Christie was very fond of Richard, but sadly he had died the year before, and so, with typical Glyndebourne hospitality, Moran Caplat gave all the boxes at Glyndebourne to Elizabeth's family for the performance. Any misgivings Elizabeth's father Fyfe, and her mother Betty had entertained concerning the age of their new son-in-law, had been expressed with true Scottish forthright-ness before the wedding, and with that welcome into the family Elizabeth became Mrs. Richard Lewis.

A unique figure in the world of opera, John Christie was a charm-ing, unpretentious man, devoted almost as much to the gardens at

Glyndebourne as to the opera house. He would spend hours tending the plants, and visitors would sometimes believe they had talked to the gardener, until they met him later in evening dress. Richard loved to tell the story of his own meeting with some overseas visitors in the garden when he was in costume for *Così fan Tutte*. John airily introduced him as the head gardener, and it seems everyone thought that this was just another Glyndebourne tradition.

The question of where they should live had occupied the couple for some time, but eventually a cottage was found and contracts exchanged on Sanctuary, Wilmington, a week before the wedding.

Following the Proms in September, Richard was booked to sing operatic rôles in Buenos Aires and Rio de Janeiro for the Wagneriana Society, and would have anticipated an interesting contrast of parts in *Idomeneo* and Janacek's *Jenufa*, but for once Richard was not looking forward to travel. Still, he could count on a tan from the South American part of his trip and a visit to Hamilton, Bermuda might be interesting. How interesting, he would discover.

Everyone dreams of an island in the sun, but few have a Robinson Crusoe existence in mind; something in between would be nice. On the one hand lots of sunshine, wonderful beaches, peace and quiet. On the other, good medical services, efficient plumbing and television. When Richard arrived in Hamilton he looked around and saw them all. As if that were not enough, it was British. A self-governing colony comprising three hundred coral islands of which twenty are inhabited; the largest is called Bermuda or Great Bermuda and the capital is Hamilton. So much for daydreaming.

There was his recital to think about and a rehearsal with a pianist new to him, but that still left time to look around and take some photographs and on his way home via New York, he would have lunch with Herbert and ask him what he thought. It did make sense. Half if not more of his work was in America. Certainly much more than half his income came from America via Herbert Barrett's office. Geographically it was perfectly situated. A tiny bit of Britain off the coast of the United States. Travel in either direction would be easy, and if the tax situation could be sorted out....

When Richard took on the rôle of Captain Vere in Benjamin

Britten's *Billy Budd*, he knew that he had found a part which suited him perfectly. Almost fifty, his maturity was obviously an asset and he looked magnificent in the naval officer's uniform of the period. But there was much more to it than this which made for perfect casting. There was something in Richard's psyche, perhaps to do with control and determination, which fitted him so well to sing Captain Vere.

In the audience was Peter Pears and he was so impressed that he sent a note to Richard's dressing room: 'Absolutely wonderful, Richard,' he wrote, with typical generosity.

Herbert was proving to be a wonderful agent, and a series of concerts beginning in New York with *Das Lied* and continuing to Adelaide for *Troilus and Cressida*, and then back again to Houston and San Francisco for three performances of Beethoven's 9th Symphony could leave Elizabeth in no doubt that she was married to a man on the move. On May 10th he would celebrate his half century, as he called it, and they would be back home in Sanctuary.

Glyndebourne and *L'incoronazione di Poppea* were to occupy May and June, and in July Richard appeared at Sadler's Wells in Handel's *Richard I* for the Handel Opera Society.

August, and *Idomeneo* at Glyndebourne, with a concert performance at the Proms on the 17th of the month made for a very busy summer. In December, in the middle of Offenbach's *Tales of Hoffmann* at Covent Garden, Richard made his second recording of *Gerontius* with Barbirolli and gave music critics and record collectors something to argue about. As previously mentioned, opinion was equally divided, and the choice is difficult. 'Sargent or Barbirolli' remains a subject for discussion thirty years later. Interestingly, Richard preferred the Sargent.

By now, Elgar's masterpiece was part of him, and he had to admit that he owed a great deal to his identification with the rôle of Gerontius. He loved singing it, and most of the time he felt uplifted by the music, but there was an exception to this. On one occasion, as he was singing the last passages of *Gerontius*, an elderly man fainted in the orchestra stalls close to the platform and had to be taken out on a stretcher. The dramatic incident was made farcical by Richard's words as he sang – 'Take me away', and orchestra, choir and audience, not to mention Sir Malcolm Sargent, did all they could to control their mixed emotions. A few days later it was reported that the man had died, and everyone was saddened by the news.

Moses and Aaron

It was called many things. From the sublime to the disgusting, but, like it or not, in 1965 it was a musical milestone of enormous importance.

In an interview with Leslie Ayre of the *London Evening News*, 14th May 1965, Georg Solti was passionate in his commitment to the work: 'I regard it, in the 20th century context, as being as great as Wagner's *Ring* – a great human drama. It has been said that the work cannot be put on the stage. I believe that it can – and that Peter Hall is the man to do it. I am enchanted with his work as producer. I think he is brilliant and I am collaborating with him with great joy. I honestly think every great opera house has a duty and obligation to play this kind of masterpiece, no matter how costly.'

Schoenberg's posthumous opera had been staged only twice before, the first time under Hans Rosbaud at Zurich being at least musically acceptable. The principal opera houses of the world had considered staging it, but the enormous difficulties inherent in the work had always led to the project being abandoned. Schoenberg's death in 1951 in Los Angeles before he could even hear it – a concert performance of some of the music took place in Germany shortly before he died – leaves it incomplete, but most agree it is complete as it is and the Cry of Moses at the end of Act 2 is a fitting conclusion.

The two principal parts were taken by Forbes Robinson as

?

Moses, a speaking part, and Richard as Aaron. To achieve a balance between the speaker and the singer was a problem initially, but only one of many problems Solti and Hall encountered. For Richard the challenge was enormous. His experience in contemporary music stood him in good stead, but he felt Aaron was the most difficult rôle he had ever sung. The complexity of the score and the demands of the high tenor writing against the massive orchestra were hard – not to mention the constant counting required.

A centrepiece of the opera is the 'Dance Round the Golden Calf', in which Schoenberg's 'realism' is pushed to its extreme limits. The composer gave the most precise stage directions as well as musical instructions, which impose a heavy burden on singers, orchestra and producer. The feverish momentum of the music demands the utmost in concentration from the musicians. The producer has to handle processions of horses, asses and camels; some with loaded wagons, making their way on stage from different entrances; followed by herds of animals awaiting the ceremonial slaughter. The arrival and departure of tribal chiefs on horseback amidst all the organised confusion and the overwhelming orchestral sound rising from the pit rivals the logistics of Trooping the Colour.

To prepare the audience for the complexities of *Moses and Aaron,* a symposium was held at Covent Garden and the press was appreciative of the way it was presented and the benefits gained. David Cairns in the *Financial Times* wrote (15th June 1965):

'The symposium was exactly as it ought to have been – relaxed and informal, purposeful and brief, well varied, giving just enough glimpse behind the scenes and explaining just enough of the technical problems to whet the appetite, conveying an impression of a dedicated effort by the whole Opera House, radiating a conviction by all concerned that this is really going to be something memorable' –

Composers Michael Tippett and William Walton bought scores and records to prepare themselves for the event, and Richard, who had taken only two days to learn Busoni's *Dr. Faustus,* had studied Aaron for four months. The foregoing gives some idea of the mammoth scale and difficulty of the opera.

Was it worth it? There were those who thought not. But in the main the critics and public applauded the decision to mount the so called impossible and said so in no unmistakable terms.

The London Music Critic of the *Liverpool Post* 29.12.65
'Meticulous preparation was clearly the healthy foundation for a galvanising enthusiasm and belief that inspired the entire company last night and resulted in a common impact from music and staging alike. This was undoubtedly a great performance of a masterpiece and for all its difficulties we must hope that it is retained in the repertoire for many years to come.'

The audience stood for more than ten minutes of continuous applause and 'bravos' and soloists, conductor and producer were rewarded with an overwhelming ovation. It was generally agreed that no other tenor in Britain could have surmounted the difficulties with such success.

Two incidents from the *Moses and Aaron* production reveal the funny and the earnest aspects in Richard's character. At a pre-dress rehearsal Richard came on stage to find a number of the maidens taking part in the orgy scene naked from the waist up. Richard seems to have been quite startled and a chorus member commented that it was the first time he had seen Richard Lewis at a loss for words. Richard finally turned to Peter Hall and, in mock exasperation, spluttered, 'You might have warned me!'

Following the first performance a number of journalists were waiting at the stage door to catch the nude dancers when Richard appeared and was quite angry with them, almost prepared to punch someone on the nose for his interest in the 'scandalous' rather than the serious nature of the opera. Fortunately Sir David Webster was right behind and persuaded Richard to leave things to him.

This reaction on the part of a very passionate man to anything suggestive may seem unusual – male opera singers are not normally noted for their delicacy in matters related to sex – but Richard's upbringing stayed with him for the whole of his life and Mary Thomas' strict Methodist attitude was an abiding influence. That said, even the theatre world was different then, and Covent

Garden's stage manager, Stella Chitty, would wait in the wings ready to cover the nude dancers the moment they exited.

Looking back thirty years to *Billy Budd* and *Moses and Aaron,* Sir Georg Solti says of Richard: 'I found him to be an excellent actor as well as the possessor of a remarkable voice. Britten was very active in this collaboration and in Captain Vere Richard gave us the essential Englishman. Years before I had conducted a Verdi *Requiem* with him and I was aware of the lovely quality of the voice, but he was also an astonishing musician. In *Moses and Aaron* he was brilliantly lyrical in this most difficult work. It was the incorporation of voice and musicianship that I appreciated so much. I found him very sympathetic, and he was always very well prepared and knew precisely the requirements of the score.'

Michael was now thirteen and, concerned for his education, Richard looked for a school not too far from London. After considering several, he settled on Aldenham and hoped Michael would be happy there. Apart from providing his son with a good education, its proximity to Heathrow made it ideal from Richard's point of view, and Mary would have more freedom with Michael at boarding school. Unfortunately, Michael didn't enjoy his time there, but it was not the school's fault that his health was making life miserable and frequent asthma attacks left him frightened and unhappy. 'I was proud of my father's reputation as a famous singer, but I didn't feel I knew him. When I was small he was always coming and going, and there was never any time. My mother had explained to me while I was still in prep school, that they would be separating and I was sad about this, but I did admire him for what he did.'

San Francisco and Los Angeles in the autumn provided the near-perfect mix of repertoire for Richard with *Die Fledermaus, Don Giovanni* and *Lulu*. After *Moses and Aaron* refreshment indeed although Alban Berg's *Lulu* was far from straightforward. Before he could go home a number of rehearsals with the Bach Aria Group for their New York Town Hall engagement in January would end his working year on just the right note. A family Christmas with Elizabeth's sister Grace and her husband Godfrey had been planned, and they could unwind and replenish their energies, spend some time with Michael – well a few days anyway – then pack their bags to return to New York on the last day of the year. There had to be an easier way to an earn a living, but not one that provided half so much fun, he decided.

The Bach Aria Group was the brainchild of a Bach enthusiast, William Scheide. A millionaire happy to invest in an ensemble of singers and instrumentalists dedicated to the performance of Bach at the highest level, Scheide was almost obsessional in his dedication to the great composer. It only required his observation of a highway sign with a number the same as a cantata, for him to start singing that particular work. The BAG members found this enthusiasm (and knowledge) initially uplifting, but after a while it became wearisome. The Group then devised ways of keeping William off the subject.

Their mandate was to perform several concerts each year in New York and additionally to tour the universities. They became a much-admired ensemble and over a period of ten years, Scheide saw his ambition to take Bach to every state in the United States fulfilled.

To sing Bach was not only musically satisfying to Richard, he saw it as recuperating for the voice and recommended it to students whenever the opportunity arose. With more *Moses and Aaron* performances scheduled for the winter months of 1966, he took full advantage of his daily dose of Bach.

That visit to Hamilton in 1964 was about to pay off. All he had learned about Bermuda then, and all he had subsequently discovered was put into effect that year. No longer would England be their base, but the sun-drenched island of Bermuda. Herbert had given his advice – accountants in London and New York had done their calculations – Mary and Michael had been well provided for – so now was the moment. Elizabeth and Richard boarded the 4.15pm flight to Hamilton from London on Sunday 28th August, and on Tuesday morning Richard took his driving test to qualify for a licence. With some local help and not a little luck, the search for a suitable house had borne fruit and their address from now on was Casuarina, Harrington Sound, Bermuda. This was the house which had so impressed Martin Isepp and which he called 'an idyllic spot'.

From Manchester to Glyndebourne is a fair journey. From Sussex to Bermuda is even further and that is not reckoning in miles. Bathed in sunshine, Richard could hardly believe his good fortune. It seemed to him that all he had ever longed for was his and Bermuda completed it. When he wasn't studying he was playing tennis. No need to worry about the weather; the sun was guaranteed. Richard might be in his element behind the wheel of a Mercedes, but these days he hopped the island on a scooter. A little heavier at fifty-two perhaps, but it was fun, and when he came off, which he did, there wasn't far to fall.

It is impossible to look at the life of Richard Lewis without being conscious of its symmetry. Until the age of twenty-five the preparation for the career. From twenty-five to fifty the development of the career. From fifty the fulfilment of the career and, parallel to this working life, his two marriages and two sons.

Nigel James Lewis was born on 30th August 1967 in Cuckfield Hospital, during the Glyndebourne season, and it would be tempting to draw the conclusion that fine musician that he was and analytical thinker almost to a fault, any failures in Richard's relationship with Michael might have been remedied with his second son – the first providing useful experience for the second. Richard could open a score and see at a glance what was going on. Where the pitfalls occurred; where the opportunities to rest were provided; where the magic could be revealed. But human beings were not predictable, and human nature was never his speciality off stage.

In case an impression has been given that Richard was not a loving father, this must be corrected without delay. We need only to look at the delightful portrait of Richard with his baby son to know how mistaken this would be. He loved Michael and Nigel very much indeed and wanted to give them every chance to grow strong and wise. If he tried too hard to put old heads on young shoulders, he will not be the first or last father to do so. If he failed to communicate in the personal terms his sons hoped for, then his failure was one he could not correct – an intrinsic part of his nature. Michael sums up the situation very clearly. 'When I was a young boy I didn't get to know him. By the time I was a teenager at school I found it hard to understand him. An example was haircuts. It was the fashion then to grow our hair long, but my father would have none of it. He thought we looked sloppy and gave a bad impression of ourselves. The fact that we were all the same didn't alter things. He had chosen to send me to a public school and he hoped it would show. He demanded so much of himself and expected so much of others, I always felt I'd let him down. When he was in his seventies I got to know him better, but it was late in the day and I regret it.'

The Edinburgh Festival once more and two of his favourite works. *A Child of Our Time* – Michael Tippett's oratorio using Negro spirituals in the manner of Bach's chorales – and Benjamin Britten's *Cantata Academica*, which was becoming a familiar friend.

Bermuda is a photographer's paradise, and Richard spent hours with camera in hand. He photographed the glorious views of sea and sand and recorded the daily growth of his new offspring. Elizabeth and Nigel were an advertising agent's delight and could have sold baby food or nappies with ease. Richard loved his life in Bermuda, and not least because of the sun. He couldn't get enough of it, and not only did he look good, but he felt well. Even the pain in his wrists and knees which he sometimes experienced in America and Europe was less severe in the warmth of Bermuda's sun, and he added golf to his sports recreations.

In contrast with the first half of his career, marriage to Elizabeth provided the support of a companion who was always at his side. More, that companion was herself a professional singer, well able to understand the stresses of vocal performance and to soothe ruffled nerves and lift flagging spirits. Frequently she acted as a go-between and dealt with situations on Richard's behalf when charm and tact were required. From Nigel's point of view the constant travelling could have proved disruptive, but Richard and Elizabeth were fortunate in the nature of their son, which, far from being upset by the changing scene, blossomed in it.

Homeward Bound

Music in Philadelphia means the symphony orchestra and the Curtis Institute. By 1968 Richard was a regular soloist with the orchestra and he grabbed every opportunity to work with his friend and mentor Eugene Ormandy. His reputation had led to an appointment as visiting Professor of Singing the year before and this was the first year of his teaching commitment at Curtis. It had been founded by Mary Louise Bok in memory of her father Cyrus Curtis in 1924, and the distinguished pianist Rudolf Serkin had just been appointed to succeed Efrem Zimbalist as Director.

Richard was a welcome addition to the teaching staff, few tenors in the world having such a rounded experience, and even fewer possessing the analytical turn of mind necessary in a good teacher. For him, the chance to work with young talent was heaven-sent and he enjoyed enormously his work there. His contract required at least ten days of five hours per day each term, but the arrangement allowed him to break the lessons where necessary to fulfil his engagements. It was without doubt, one of the most privileged teaching appointments in the world of music, and his students gained greatly from their no nonsense, plain speaking teacher. Explaining is one thing, demonstrating another. On one occasion Richard paid for taxis to transport a group of students to a concert he was giving in order that they could see him put into practice what he was teaching.

Everyone who came to know Richard well was impressed by

his loyalty which seemed to remain unchanging whatever the circumstances. Relationships were not entered into lightly and friendship was not something handed out to anyone who happened to be around. On the other hand 'once a friend then always a friend' was a phrase that could be employed to describe him. Leopold Simoneau, Marjorie Thomas and Eugene Ormandy were members of a group Richard regarded as friends; Mary Lewis was another. His diary always noted her birthday and he never failed to send a card. Of course they shared an ongoing interest in Michael, but there was more to it than that, and Richard was loyal to an old friend who was once his wife.

Throughout the sixties and seventies, Richard was spending a good deal of time in the recording studio and unlike many singers whose voices record less well, or, conversely, record excitingly but are disappointing in concert, he sounded equally convincing in either situation. In 1969 his *Elijah* recording for RCA with the Philadelphia Orchestra under Ormandy was memorable, as was his Herod in *Salomé* with the London Symphony Orchestra under Erich Leinsdorf. This star-studded cast included Caballé, Milnes, Resnick and King. In 1970 he was back with Ormandy for Beethoven's *Missa Solemnis* in the company of Martina Arroyo, Maureen Forrester and Cesare Siepi.

There was in the timbre of Richard's voice a quality which is impossible to describe in words. Above all it was brave. Not brave in the sense that he tackled passages which demanded courage – his war cry in *King Priam* for example – but brave in terms of the sound produced. An inspirational attribute present in Bjoerling and Corelli, which is at once strong and vulnerable. When Richard sang he was sharing a gift with others. In a very real way he saw it as an obligation. His song in the woods of Sand Hutton was shared with Richard Colclough. His offer to sing to Geoffrey Parsons' father was another example. In 1971 Richard was in Chicago for *Moses and Aaron* and Alan Rothnie, Britain's Consul General, invited him to dinner. During the meal Anne Rothnie mentioned a young diplomat who was ill in hospital with a nervous breakdown. Richard was spontaneous in his reaction to the news. Would the young man like Richard to sing to him, he asked? 'Sometimes music helps when nothing else will,' he added. The Rothnies never forgot the generosity of Richard's gesture. 'He seemed remote to people who didn't know him,' Lady Rothnie told me, 'yet there was a caring side which was so touching when it appeared.'

Sharing for Richard extended to singing to the natives of Hoo Hui in Argentina after a visit to the Festival of the Virgin. Richard was appearing at the Teatro Colón in Buenos Aires and had taken Elizabeth with him. The British Council had arranged a day trip and they were on their way back in the evening. Coming across a group of natives sitting around a camp fire the BC representative explained who Richard was and a song was requested. Elizabeth remembers, as if it were yesterday, the faces of the men in the firelight as they listened to 'Come Back to Sorrento'!

On a very personal note, Elizabeth was adept in those small things that make a big difference in life, and if for instance a manicure or pedicure was needed, she was on hand to perform these delicate services. Richard was immaculate in his person to an unusual degree – it would have run counter to his aesthetic sense to be otherwise – and Elizabeth was quite expert with comb and scissors, replacing the barbers he had regularly visited before.

The move to Bermuda five years earlier had made a world of difference for the singer who was sometimes referred to by the press as 'Britain's dollar-earning tenor'. Without the convenience of Bermuda, this would have been quite impossible, and yet the stress of so much travel had increased the frequency and severity of the pain in his limbs, which by this time had been diagnosed as rheumatoid arthritis. How many times had friends and family expressed concern over his lifestyle? He had lost count. Now the specialists he consulted about his aches and pains were saying the same thing, but then everyone knew doctors exaggerated. He felt fine most of the time and the voice was as good as ever; that was a sign, surely. He must take off a few pounds and relax more; that would do the trick.

His rôle of Eumete in the 1972 production of *Il Ritorno d'Ulisse* at Glyndebourne may have been in part a recognition of his need to relax a little. Monteverdi's opera had first been produced in Sussex in Raymond Leppard's edition some years before when Richard was busy with *Idomeneo* and *Fidelio*: now, the chance to sing the old shepherd was just the way to ease himself back into Glyndebourne after an absence of five years. There was talk of *Idomeneo* in 1974 and if that were the case, who else could they ask?

Nigel was going to be five in August and there was his schooling to consider. With *King Priam* at Covent Garden in May side by side with *Il Ritorno d'Ulisse* at Glyndebourne, perhaps this was the time to return to England. All things considered it wasn't a bad idea, and it would give him a chance to discuss his arthritis with someone in Harley Street. There was also Michael to think about, as well as Vera and Gwyneth and friends such as Elizabeth's sister, Grace and brother-in-law Godfrey; these considerations apart, there was a strong feeling of homesickness. A longing for England and things English. Cricket at the Oval and tea at Fortnum's.

Before she said goodbye to Bermuda, Elizabeth was able to realise some further musical ambitions and sang with Richard several times. 'It was an exhilarating experience,' she recalls. 'I had learnt so much from him over the years, that when we appeared as fellow professionals he was wonderfully encouraging and appreciative of my work. The high point must have been our collaboration in *Gerontius*, when I sang the Angel. The setting in Washington Cathedral was perfect, and the National Symphony under Paul Callaway, provided excellent support. It made everything we had worked for worthwhile.' The reviews in the *Washington Post* and the *Star* on 27th March must have pleased the husband and wife team. Paul Hume wrote:

' Elizabeth Lewis, who is the tenor's wife, proved a notable mezzo in the rôle of Guardian Angel, projecting both tenderness and a fine breadth where needed. She sang with a tone of singular polish.'

And Irving Lowens in the *Star* said,

'The glow and patina in Lewis's voice could have been predicted, but I must confess that his wife's mastery of oratorio and her utterly exquisite singing came as a very pleasant surprise.'

Richard had always kept in touch with his sister and Gwyneth, and just before Glyndebourne opened in 1972, Ibbs and Tillett arranged a recital in Macclesfield which prompted him to stay with Gwyneth and her husband Eric Mitchell. Gwyneth – or 'little Gwyneth', as Richard always thought of her – was one of his favourite people, and he told her about his plans for the future. For Vera, Richard's return must have been very welcome news as the annual visits she had customarily paid to her brother before he left to live in Bermuda could now be resumed. Among their closest friends were Harold Ford and his wife, another Vera. Harold was a Methodist minister – close to Richard in the CPA days – who offici-ated at his marriage to Elizabeth in Brighton and was probably his oldest friend. In the course of time Harold died and Vera married Elizabeth's father, Fyfe, who was a widower ... but that was still in the future.

Another home, but this time on familiar Sussex ground, White Acre was in Forest Row and ideally located for Glyndebourne and London. Once again Elizabeth's decorating skills would be brought into play, and the search for a school for Nigel begun.

In May Richard celebrated his sixtieth birthday and his diary reveals something of his attitude to reaching this particular mile-stone. *'60th Birthday!'* he notes on 10th May. Some time later with a different pen in hand he scored through the 60 and wrote 49!!! It is how we all feel, presumably, but there is something in the writing which refuses to accept the situation.

Judged in the light of his earlier years, Richard was not so busy. *Idomeneo* at Glyndebourne and *Jephtha* for the Handel Opera Soci-ety at Sadler's Wells were his principal engagements. When did he first sing 'Waft Her Angels', he wondered? He looked back over the years to a lesson with Norman Allin. Was it possible? So much time, so many places. He did it differently then, but he was different then. Not Richard Lewis even, just plain Tom Thomas.

Conducting an orchestra has been called the ultimate in control, consequently we should not be surprised at Richard's interest in the discipline. It is certain that he saw himself in the rôle of conductor and considered he could do no worse, and probably a lot better, than many under whom he had been obliged to sing. His chance came with a performance of *Gerontius* which was well received and his reading must have been a fascinating fusion of all he considered best in Sargent and Barbirolli. Richard would have welcomed the opportunity to conduct more, but the pain in his arms and shoulders inhibited movement and left him depressed. On this occasion Gerontius was sung by Anthony Rolfe Johnson, whom many regard as Richard's successor in the rôle.

Recalling these times, Anthony Rolfe Johnson says. 'I worked with Richard on a number of occasions as a student and as a colleague, and was lucky enough to perform *Gerontius* with Richard conducting. This meant that I was privy to his own inner view of that rôle, and I felt myself privileged to be there and taking part in that performance. History was being made: it was a wonderful opportunity for a young singer to sing Elgar's music under the baton of the greatest exponent of that rôle, on disk or live. His performances were definitive, and are still the benchmark for all young tenors. This is the rôle which everyone will remember him by.'

Among Richard's reasons for returning to England was a strong desire to pass on the benefits of his long experience, to teach others what he had learned. The Curtis Institute had been very sorry to see him go, and had made various proposals to keep him on the faculty, but he and they knew it was not practical. Austin University was one of several music colleges which tried to secure his services around this time, but which he had to turn down for the same reason. Now he hoped that the Royal Academy would ask him to join them, and in the meantime his old association the Incorporated Society of Musicians needed him on the council. It was not long before the word got around that Richard was back in England and several potential students contacted him with a view to private lessons. This was not exactly what he had envisaged, but whether in a room at the RAM, or at home in Forest Row, it was still teaching and provided the student was of a sufficiently high standard, Richard was pleased to help. Over the next few years a number of Richard's students gained entry into the profession and his influence remains with them. One such was Michael Preston-Roberts, who found Richard 'really easy to get on with and very warm on occasion. He was a caring teacher,' Michael says, 'and only too willing to reduce his fees when he knew I couldn't manage. Later, when I sang under Kenneth Alwyn, Richard came to the concert. It included "Onaway Awake" and I was full of trepidation, but I needn't have been. He was very generous in his praise of my performance.' About practice repertoire Richard was clear-cut in his instruction. 'When you are going through a bad patch get out your Bach, Handel and Mozart; it will come right again, I promise you!'

The casting of *Idomeneo* at Glyndebourne in 1974 found Richard sharing the rôle with George Shirley, and according to the majority of the reviewers, holding his own. As Alan Blyth commented in the autumn issue of Opera, Richard's performance was 'at once authoritative and deeply moving.' Not a bad return for a man of sixty.

His intention to seek more medical advice took him to the Royal Homoeopathic Hospital as well as to Harley Street in a search for relief from his arthritis, but the answers he received served to confuse rather than relieve.

Elizabeth was a great support at this stage, encouraging Richard to take more rest and to consider carefully the engagements he took on. Another *Messiah*, *Gerontius* or *St. Matthew Passion* was much less important than a free day to recharge his batteries. Wasn't that one of the reasons for which they had returned home?

The problem from Richard's viewpoint was different. He had returned to England after a long absence and he believed he must do everything offered to re-establish himself. In the meantime the next generation of tenors had matured and other names were now thought of where Richard Lewis would have previously been the automatic choice. That this situation would have occurred anyway, and that it was time for the senior man to ease up, went against the grain. To age gracefully was to relinquish control, and that had never been his way.

As tennis was no longer possible for painful knees and wrists, Richard turned more and more to golf as a recreation. The doctors said exercise and movement were important in the treatment of rheumatic conditions and the walking the game involved should help. The problem was, he had taken it up late in life and the rotation of hips and knees, not to mention the impact of club and ball, were certainly unhelpful to inflamed joints. Elizabeth pondered the pros and cons, but any reminder of the advance of time was anathema to her determined husband, so for the moment she held her peace.

Nigel was now seven and getting used to being in England. He had never known so many miserable days without sun, and instead of life revolving around the beach, people kept talking about the importance of school and which school was the best. His father was at home more, but sometimes he was in a bad mood and obviously in pain.

More doctors and more medicine, and then the big decision was made. Richard would have surgery immediately after Christmas to replace his right hip, and the hope was that this would make walking very much easier. On19th December 1974, he entered the Esperance Private Hospital in Eastbourne. Of course he was worried about his future mobility and how this would affect his movement on stage, but his concern was unnecessary. A relatively straightforward operation, the first results were very encouraging and his nineteen days in hospital were as good as such visits can ever be. The nursing staff were excellent and he noted how attentive Sisters Patricia, Heclan and Clotilde were. It was not the dreadful experience he had anticipated, and he made a quick recovery. The letters and phone calls from friends in the profession were enormously reassuring and dispelled any thoughts that he had been forgotten. Among the messages was one from Sylvia Darley, Sir Malcolm Sargent's secretary for many years and now running the cancer fund named after him. She sent a bottle of old whisky which she hoped he would enjoy once the doctors gave the okay. Just six weeks later Richard was singing at the Paris Opera.

Still Dreaming

In a year when he might have expected to do less, he was extremely busy. He had been elected President of the ISM, and performed the duties of that office, with meetings of the various sections such as the Solo Performers and Private Teachers, and travel to the different centres of the Society in Manchester, Birmingham, Liverpool and Sheffield, taking up a fair amount of his time. In fact Richard loved administration and was well suited to it. Indeed, his presidency saw a change in the building used by the ISM, and the establishment of the Gold Medal for Achievement. Everyone who knew Richard felt this last to be entirely in keeping with the character of the man.

Productions at the Paris Opera included *Moses and Aaron* and *Electra,* concerning which there is an amusing story. At the time, Paris was subject to a great deal of industrial unrest and terrorist activity, and power failures were commonplace. During *Electra*, in which Birgit Nielsen was appearing, the lights went out and the opera came to a dramatic halt. Every effort was made to restore the electricity and eventually this was successful. By chance, Richard was required to resume singing with the line 'Lights. Lights. Is there no one here to light them?' (*trans.*), which caused the audience to dissolve into hysterical laughter.

At Covent Garden there was *King Priam*, and, in between Paris and London, a flying visit to Rome to sing *Messiah* with the Santa Cecilia Orchestra. Canada was freezing in November when he sang

Gerontius in Ottawa, but he was back in time for visits from Vera, who was celebrating her seventieth birthday and from Beryl and Richard Colclough who came for a short holiday. All in all, a busy schedule for a man with a new hip.

Elizabeth was now doing a considerable amount of singing and was represented by Ibbs and Tillett, Richard's first agents. Apart from concerts and broadcasting, she collaborated with the London Festival Ballet in de Falla's *Three Cornered Hat*, which proved to be a delightful experience. She also lectured on music at Sussex University, which she much enjoyed.

One of the few conductors to emerge from the world of singing, James Paul was Associate Conductor of the Milwaukee Symphony when Richard sang with them in 1978. Like Richard, a tenor, James Paul had first heard Richard on records when he was working in a music shop while a student at the Oberlin Conservatory and, as he recalls 'I was knocked out! The first chance I had to hear him in the flesh was when he came to sing *Gerontius* with Boston's Handel-Haydn Orchestra under Edwin F. Gilday. I had heard Sargent's recording of course and I was enormously impressed with Richard and this introduction to Edward Elgar. I went to the dressing rooms afterwards – Marjorie Thomas and Forbes Robinson were the other soloists – and congratulated everyone. It was then that I vowed to myself that I would conduct *Gerontius* one day with Richard singing. Four years later this ambition was fulfilled, but by this time he was sixty-seven and I wondered how it would be. In the rehearsal break my colleague, Margaret Hawkins, Chorus Director of the Milwaukee Choir, came hurrying round to see me. "Isn't he wonderful?" she said – "You can hear every word, no matter how loud the orchestra is."'

Paul believes that Richard had, and continues to have, a great influence on him as a conductor. 'He was certainly Britain's greatest tenor and among the best in the world, but he was not always as tactful as he might have been. When rehearsing Bach's *St. Matthew Passion* with William Steinberg for instance, Richard sat shaking his head sadly until Steinberg stopped the orchestra and demanded what was wrong. Without hesitation he answered – 'Too much rubato.' Steinberg couldn't believe his ears and asked the question again. 'Too much rubato,' replied Richard. 'It was as simple as that,' says James Paul. 'The music was more important than anything else.'

James Paul also speaks with admiration of Richard's musical consistency. 'The broadcaster, Jim Unrath was presenting a music programme "Lincoln's Music" for the station WFMT prior to a performance of *Gerontius* under Sir Colin Davis. Unrath had taken "Sanctus Fortis" in three recordings by Sargent, Barbirolli and myself, and spliced them together almost seamlessly. It was amazing to hear how Richard had maintained voice and style in each excerpt over more than twenty years.'

Another *Gerontius*, this time under Andrew Davis, was of the greatest importance to Richard, who at sixty-six, was wondering just how much longer his precious gift could last; he was not alone. The Philharmonic Hall in Liverpool was packed for the Royal Liverpool Philharmonic Orchestra and Chorus, with Sarah Walker and Rodney MacAnn as the other soloists. Elizabeth was in the audience and as anxious as her husband, but when she arrived in the Green Room at the interval she was surprised to find him in tears because she knew he had sung as well as ever. 'Is everything all right?' she asked. Richard took her in his arms and whispered in her ear, 'I can still do it.' He held her tight for some time, overcome with emotion.

Neil Barkla reviewed the concert the following day (26.11.80) under the headline 'The Complete Dream'. After praise for Andrew Davis and the other soloists, he wrote:

'The return of Richard Lewis in the rôle which he has sung for so many years showed him still without a peer.'

Nigel was now thirteen and ready to sit the Common Entrance examination for entry to a public school. His time at Cumnor Preparatory School had been successful and he was very much involved in the musical life of the school, leading the orchestra on several occasions. As Herbert Barrett had observed, Richard placed great store by education and wanted his boys to have the best available.

Nigel says: 'My father was a perfectionist and some of that eventually rubbed off on me, but at the time, being taught by one was very difficult. He tried to show me his affection, but I've always felt his own upbringing got in the way.'

His diaries for Michael's and Nigel's years at school are filled with reminders to attend concerts and plays, as well as the traditional end of year days and sports fixtures. It is clear he wanted to be involved, and perhaps not just for his sons' sakes. There is a feeling that he too is taking part, enjoying belatedly a school life that his parents could never provide. No doubt the consequence of this was the pressure he placed on them to do well. Nigel's success in the Common Entrance came as a relief to Elizabeth and Richard and secured him a place at Eastbourne College. It was as a result of this that they decided to move from Forest Row to Willingdon.

With several golf clubs close at hand, Combe House seemed the perfect choice and Richard was happy to think that his moving days were over. His seventieth birthday was not far off and if there were still a few concerts left in him – and that last *Gerontius* suggested that there were – then so be it. All the same he knew he must be prepared to hang up his boots, or whatever tenors did, in a year or two. He would cross that bridge when he came to it. In June, Madrid should be beautiful and he was looking forward to singing four *Electra*s there.

San Francisco still wanted him for *Wozzeck* in November and Elizabeth would join him. After that he was due to sing *On Wenlock Edge* and Britten's *Serenade* for Radio Hilversum in December. Not his busiest year (1981), but busy enough. In between a lot was going on and a good friend, the conductor Janet Canetty-Clarke invited him to sing a *St. Matthew Passion* in which Elizabeth was also involved. The Ditchling Choral Society is a distinguished body established in 1921, and making a significant contribution to music in the south of England. Under Janet Canetty-Clarke the choir has undertaken a wide repertoire and gained an enviable reputation for the meticulous preparation and authenticity of the work offered.

Richard had first sung with them in 1975 when the performance was also devoted to the *St. Matthew Passion*, and Janet recalls vividly the impact of his delivery at that moment of utter despair –

'and all His disciples forsook Him and fled.' 'I shall never forget it,' she says. The following year, Richard 'borrowed' the choir for the performance he directed of *Gerontius* with Anthony Rolfe Johnson, and Janet found the discussion in rehearsal between the two tenors 'a lesson in itself for me'.

In 1980 Richard sang in the first performance of Howard Blake's *Benedictus* which the Choral Society commissioned, and which has enjoyed frequent performance in many countries since that première with the National Philharmonic Orchestra. Richard's idea to use spoken words against the orchestra in the central section of the work was acknowledged an inspiration by the composer.

Janet speaks with great affection for Richard, whose willingness to help the choir at this stage in his career was unstinting. No doubt he remembered his own choir at the Methodist church in Manchester so many years before. One of Janet's treasured memories concerns the performance she conducted of Britten's *War Requiem* with the Philharmonia Orchestra in 1989. 'Richard talked me through the work,' she says, 'and attended the concert in Worth Abbey with Elizabeth. That was a special evening.'

In February 1982 Richard sang in Britten's *Spring Symphony* with the Concertgebouw in Amsterdam and recalled his first appearances with that great orchestra under Eduard van Beinum more than thirty years before. What a wonderful hall, the Concertgebouw, and what splendid acoustics. One concert stood out in his memory, when he sang Mahler's *Das Lied von der Erde*, with the fine contralto, Eugenia Zareska, a colleague from Glyndebourne. There was that name again. Were those last performances of *Il Ritorno d'Ulisse* in 1979 to be his swan song? Well, his record was going to be hard to beat: three hundred and fourteen performances in twelve different rôles. Only old Hugues Cuénod was likely to do it. He would miss the dressing for the part. The slow change of persona with each garment added and every dab of the make-up sponge. He liked to think of himself as a singer/actor or even actor/singer. There was never any doubt regarding his vocal acting. Every nuance and character suggestion was there to be heard. Perhaps his stage movement was a bit stiff in the early days, but he had worked at it and his Rakewell and Vere were finally regarded as profound psychological studies. Dear Kay. He called her 'Mama' sometimes for fun. How many sandwiches did she wrap in a damp cloth for his long drive back to Rickmansworth, so tired when he arrived that he was asleep in seconds? Best purchase he ever made, that German car. Just like their opera houses, a bit heavy going, but utterly reliable.

He had to go into hospital for a few checks soon. The hip was working all right, but the rest of him felt a bit rusty. All those steroids they kept giving him were supposed to keep him running smoothly, but he liked the physiotherapy better. That girl whose name he could never remember.

By 1983 Richard was forced to accept the fact that his opera and concert career had come to an end and his hoped-for teaching appointment hadn't materialised. He was still a much respected and admired figure in the music world and his master classes and talks on opera were enthusiastically received, but as a singer, the end of his career had finally arrived. Some men and women are happy to accept the inevitable and continue to be seen in the milieus where their reputations have been made, and Richard went to Glyndebourne and Covent Garden from time to time, but he found the half smiles of recognition irritating rather than heart warming. The fact was, he hated not being able to sing any more and his resentment was readily felt by those close to him. The elder statesman was not a rôle for which he was by nature well suited, although he valued enormously the honours which had come his way. His doctorates from St. Andrews and Manchester meant a great deal, for it had been part of his ambition to gain a D. Mus. as a young man in Manchester before the war, although he never imagined that his degree would be bestowed *honoris causa*. He was also proud to be a FRAM and FRMCM, and knew how much he owed to both conservatories.

Richard's seventieth birthday party was an occasion of great happiness and attended by some forty guests with whom he had been associated during his long career. Most appropriately, it was held at Glyndebourne and was a surprise which Elizabeth had contrived to keep secret. An invitation to have drinks with George and Mary Christie was the bait necessary to get Richard to Glyndebourne and once they had been welcomed at the door they were led to a room where everyone was waiting. Sir Georg Solti came forward to embrace him and then everyone joined in singing 'Happy Birthday'. There were speeches from Moran Caplat, Harold Rosenthal and Wilfred Stiff, and Richard responded with stories of his early years at Glyndebourne. A splendid dinner was provided by Glyndebourne Festival Opera, to which the following were also invited: Mr and Mrs Brian Dickie, Sir John Tooley, Mr Geoffrey Parsons, Sir Alan Rothnie and Delia Rothnie, Mr and Mrs. George Christie, Mr Geoffrey Gilbertson, Mr Erich Whittier, Miss June Dandridge, Miss Janet Moores, Mr and Mrs Guy Gravett, Mr and Mrs. Frederick Fuller, Mr Peter Canetty-Clarke, Simone Canetty-Clarke, Mr and Mrs Martin Isepp, Mr and Mrs Martin Carr, Mrs Wilfred Stiff, Miss Beryl Ball, Mr Tony Tweedale, Mrs Harold Rosenthal, Mr Michael Lewis and Mr Nigel Lewis.

There were messages from many who wished to be there but were prevented for one reason or another, including Luciano Pavarotti, Sir John Pritchard, Pierrette and Leopold Simoneau, Brenda and Geraint Evans, John Shirley-Quirk, Elsie and Rafael Kubelik, Peter Andry and 'everyone at EMI', Herbert and Betty Barrett, Forbes Robinson, Kurt Herbert Adler, Ibbs and Tillett, Sena Jurinac, Lord Harewood, John McKay.

Luciano Pavarotti's letter to Elizabeth is particularly touching:

March 23rd

Dear Elizabeth

Thank you for your very kind invitation for your celebration on May 12th. I would love to attend and congratulate Richard, but at that time I am appearing in Vienna in Aida. Please give him my very best wishes for his birthday and also my feelings of appreciation on his forty years of wonderful singing.

With warm regards,

and a handwritten note at the end reads:

Luciano to Richard
"You are a great inspiration."

The event was well covered by the press during the following days, Peterborough in the *Daily Telegraph* quoting from Richard's speech of reply. Richard recalled his first *Rape of Lucretia* and the anxiety which caused him to muff his first line. Instead of 'Rome is now ruled by the Etruscan upstart' he substituted 'Rome is now ruled by the Italian dustcart.' The audience may have been amused, but by all accounts Benjamin Britten wasn't.

Seeing doctors, both orthodox and less orthodox, as well as checking in and out of hospital for tests was becoming a habit; rather like the servicing of his Mercedes. The difference was, his beloved 220S Convertible had finally been handed in for a newer model, whereas he had to make do with the body he'd got. Conventional in many ways, when it came to his health Richard was prepared to try anyone or anything in an effort to reduce his pain and Elizabeth teased him gently about his different specialists and tendency to hypochondria, a condition not exactly rare among performers.

Act 3

It was towards the end of 1984 that Richard suffered the first dramatic breakdown of his circulatory system. Due to give a talk in Brighton, he made his way to the garage where he collapsed beside the car. At work in the kitchen Elizabeth was expecting to hear him start up and wondered why he was taking so long. She sensed something might be wrong and went to the garage where she found him. He was unable to speak a word, but could stand with help and slowly they returned indoors. The doctor was called and without hesitation diagnosed a stroke.

Devastating news for anyone, it was a particularly bitter pill for such a brilliant communicator and although he slowly recovered his speech he was never the same again.

Stroke trauma very often leaves the patient physically impaired, but in Richard's case there was no paralysis and the damage was entirely mental. For example, he could not remember the Lord's Prayer, and no amount of trying helped. It would have been possible to relearn it, but Richard was embittered by what had happened and was unwilling to try. How could God have robbed him of those precious words, depriving him of their comfort just when they were most needed?

The slow process of rehabilitation began and he subjected himself to the demanding exercises necessary to reactivate his speech. One frustrating, but very amusing, incident occurred when the speech therapist assigned to work with him asked if he could try to sing a little. She had no idea who he was and spoke about melody as if to a small child. The look on Richard's face obliged Elizabeth to explain hurriedly that this particular patient knew something about singing. Later it transpired that the therapist was about to ask him to sing *Baa Baa Black Sheep*, and was extremely grateful for Elizabeth's intervention. In fact, Richard never lost his musical faculties.

Vera was expected for a short holiday, and Elizabeth believed Richard's recovery could be aided by the presence of his sister. They had shared so much as children and perhaps Vera's memories would serve to stimulate the gaps in his memory. Vera's annual visits with her husband had continued after David's death in 1972, and were times Richard looked forward to keenly. They did not always agree, but there was a special bond between them which reached back to Baden Street. Only children could never know this support, and Richard was always happy that the sons of his two marriages had a brother in one another.

Michael and Nigel were both musical, but Michael's love for the piano had been more for the instrument itself and eventually he trained as a technician before joining Steinways. Today he is one of the country's leading piano consultants with his own firm in London. Nigel, on the other hand, was drawn to the violin and did well enough to become leader of Cumnor House and Eastbourne College orchestras. His talent would have taken him into the profession, but he was equally attracted to journalism – possibly inherited from his grandfather Fyfe – and that interest won the day.

Many would regard his retirement as well-deserved and comfortable – his health apart – but performer that he was, Richard was lost without a stage, and an audience was his source of nourishment. Relatives like Grace and Godfrey lived nearby at Seaford, and Willingdon was home to an old colleague Frederick Fuller, as well as to Norman and Joan Carr and Brenda Webb, who was sometimes a holiday companion. This group of people came to mean so much to him.

Combe House was home, but much more than that. A room for Elizabeth's and Richard's singing lessons; a small gallery for photographs and paintings – the original designs for his costumes

– and finally the administrative centre for the Camerata Concert Series and Combe Arts Club, two initiatives of Elizabeth's. Brenda was a particularly close friend who assisted with these welcome additions to Eastbourne's cultural life and enjoyed her occasional holidays with the Lewises. An attractive, warm-hearted woman, she was just the sort of person to make the company of three seem preferable to two, and she was a great support to Elizabeth on many occasions when Richard was unwell. 'He was not an easy patient,' she says. 'He resented the changes in his life brought about by the end of his career. In a way this marked the end of life in the way he wished to live it. All the same, he still continued to behave like the Richard we remembered. When we had a party and were engaged in parlour games, he still played with all the seriousness he had previously shown. He could not give less than a hundred per cent to any activity and this intensity sometimes made people uncomfortable.'

Speaking with Brenda and other friends, Richard was always quite definite that his career could not have developed the way that it did, or indeed have lasted so long, without Elizabeth. Few concert artists have been blessed with this kind of devoted support, and he was eager to acknowledge it. Indeed, what man would not be grateful for this kind of helpmate? Brenda continues:

'Another example was dancing. If he danced a fox-trot or waltz his rhythm was perfect, as you might expect, but the steps were entirely of his own making. I complained to Elizabeth about this and she laughed. It had taken her years to learn the Lewis method. In so many ways he was a law unto himself.'

Now that he could no longer work, the need to fill his time productively became all important and in the search for a recreation beyond that supplied by the radio and television, Richard turned to painting. In this he was aided by an experienced teacher, Irene Bishop, who was fully understanding of his problems following a stroke as her own husband had suffered similarly. 'Richard had considerable talent with the brush, and needed only to be "freed" to paint really well. I thought he was much too controlled and over-disciplined: a perfectionist in ways that worked against the best interest of the painting. He had all the sensitivity needed, it was just a question of freeing the man. I shall never forget his great kindness, and the rapport we established meant a great deal to me.' Judging by the paintings completed, Irene helped him to achieve the freedom she speaks of and, coincidentally, relieved some of his pain.

Another diversion came as a surprise to Combe House's visitors. For a number of years, Richard had been fascinated with model railways and he attended several exhibitions in London. With the enthusiasm of a schoolboy he would spend happy hours playing with his engines, carriages and track, mindful no doubt of his father's work as a railwayman and his own roots in Manchester.

With August's good weather, and feeling a little better, Richard set out to explore his family roots in Wales. In the company of Elizabeth, Vera, Gwyneth, Michael, his wife Huilee and Nigel, he visited the cottage where his mother was born in Llas Bach. They knocked at the door and when the owner discovered who they were, she invited them in for tea and made them very welcome. She didn't need to be told who Richard Lewis was, but she wasn't expecting him to knock on her door. As they left, they noticed many bits of leather mixed in with the stones of the pathway and Richard became silent and was obviously moved. He stopped to examine a piece and then explained to the group that his grandfather had been a cobbler by trade. Their hostess was delighted to have an answer to the question she had asked herself a hundred times.

Elizabeth's sister Grace Robertson has found success in the world of photography and speaks of her brother-in-law with great affection. Living close by, Grace and Godfrey saw a lot of the Lewises, and when Richard had another stroke and Elizabeth was away from home working, Grace went to Eastbourne to take care of him while waiting for the doctor and ambulance to arrive. 'I believe he thought I was Elizabeth, as our voices are so similar, and it may have comforted him.'

She looks back: 'I saw him in the opera house many times, but I particularly remember his Florestan at Glyndebourne on the day he married Elizabeth. I've never heard the dungeon scene sung so well and I'm sure Elizabeth was his inspiration. It was heartbreaking to see this talented man cut down by illness.' Godfrey Thurston

Hopkins is another name in photography, and he recalls a session with Richard at Covent Garden when he and Geraint Evans were singing in *Die Zauberflöte* under Klemperer. 'The way these two played the fool off stage during the performance, only to switch back to their characters when they went on again amazed me. Richard was as bad as Geraint and didn't need much encouragement. It was another side to him entirely.'

With his wife's growing list of engagements, the arrival of the Carrs next door was a blessing and Richard began to drop in when he was feeling lonely for a bite of supper and a chat. He would entertain them with stories from his career, and the fact that they were not knowledgeable in a professional sense worried him not at all. With them, Richard found the warmth and companionship he needed and Elizabeth could relax a little knowing there were good neighbours close at hand. Over the years Norman and Joan became almost second parents to Elizabeth.

By 1990 Richard had aged considerably, although on good days it was commented that he looked less than his seventy-six years; but the accumulated stress of a long career could not be kept at bay any longer. His effort to fill his days as described was becoming increasingly difficult, and only weekend visits from Michael and Nigel and news of their successful careers cheered him significantly. Michael's marriage to Huilee, a lovely Malaysian Chinese girl in 1989 had given him a new lease of life, and to attend the ceremony with Mary and Elizabeth was a sure sign that any wounds had healed. Mary's own second marriage to James Kellock had been extremely happy, and the two old friends were able to meet and share their son's happiness.

Richard's painting began as a therapeutic recreation and eased the excruciating pain which sometimes racked his shoulders and arms; nevertheless it finally became an accomplishment of which he could be proud. The medication he had taken over many years had unfortunately produced side effects which were difficult to reconcile with any benefits gained, although he firmly believed that the pain control procedures of Dr. Joan Hester in Eastbourne had been of great help.

One evening when they were together watching the television, the news came that Leonard Bernstein had died. They listened to the report and the announcer ended by saying that Bernstein was seventy-two. Richard turned to Elizabeth and in a very matter of fact voice said, 'And I shall be seventy-six.' Elizabeth was shocked by the conviction of his prophecy and told Richard not to talk in that way. She was angry and frightened.

October passed uneventfully, and he was enlivened by a visit from the boys, but by the end of the month he was feeling very poorly and the gaps in his memory were worrying him. Elizabeth looked back over six months of rapid deterioration and, recalling his morbid statement, was upset and tried to put it out of her mind.

At the beginning of November, Richard agreed to be moved to a more convenient room as the struggle up and down every day was becoming a dreadful ordeal and it would make looking after him that much easier. The stress on Elizabeth during those weeks of constant care was hard, and in her heart she knew that Richard would not leave his bed again. Michael and Nigel came for a week-end and were shocked and saddened by their father's condition. A vibrant, powerful man reduced to this.

There was nothing special about the evening of the twelfth, but when Elizabeth made him comfortable for the night and kissed him, Richard looked deep into her eyes and wordlessly conveyed his gratitude and love. She was profoundly touched by the message and went to her room, exhausted, to sleep. In the morning when she went to wake him, she knew at once that he had gone. 'There was no sign of struggle and his face was at rest.'

* * * * *

During his last years Elizabeth suggested frequently that Richard should write his autobiography, but she could never get him to do more than say he would think about it. His reluctance to do so may seem strange in view of his carefully preserved diaries and notices, but I suspect there were many unresolved questions concerning his childhood and his relationship with his mother, and Richard was too honest to fudge these issues. The clearly defined, somewhat rigid terms in which he viewed the world left little room for ambiguity, and he who has a problem with the ambiguous should stay away from psychology, personal or otherwise. His great achievement in music sprang from the clarity of his vision. The heroic appeal in the 'Sanctus Fortis' from *Gerontius* leaves no room for doubt and even the desperately sad 'I can no more' from the same work is a statement of fact, not of question.

The obituaries were appropriate for a man who had given so much to the world of music and the columns of the London and New York *Times* expressed their appreciation for his gifts unstintingly. More impressive, I find, is the letter of one of Richard's many admirers, Joy Smith, who wrote as follows:

'I went out and bought the Sargent recording of *Gerontius*. Listening to it for the first time, I had a feeling that my life would be changed – which it was. I remember that for days afterwards I drove round Oxfordshire in the course of my work, feeling not entirely in this world. It has remained for me the supreme musical experience and a profoundly spiritual one. It is interesting that someone such as I, with no musical talent, should have been so inspired by Richard's art. It was both the interpretation and the tone of voice, rich, mellow, pure and the wonderful command of *sotto voce* in *Gerontius*. The decrescendos to *pppp* of "Into thy hands....." was so perfect that one could not tell at what point the voice stopped.

'This, perhaps more than any other quality was what made him such a great artist. The quiet, ethereal sound that made the audience hold its breath lest it should break the spell. At moments like that one could paraphrase St. John the Divine: "I listened and behold, a door was opened in Heaven."'

Huilee gave birth to a boy on 4th February 1995. Michael announced that Richard's grandson would be called Thomas Zhen Lewis.

Curtain Up

If all good things must come to an end, then presumably, this is a necessary law of nature, in order that other good things may begin.

When Richard died in 1990, he left behind him, in the minds of the many thousands who heard him sing, a legacy of musical memories which would be difficult to overestimate, for he was unquestionably one of the most important artists of the second half of the twentieth century. Indeed, his influence on music in Britain following the Second World War was arguably greater than that of any other singer, and the observations of Phillip Langridge and James Paul were repeated to me again and again during my research for this book.

As for that influence in the United States, the comment by Alan Rich in his review of *Billy Budd* at the Carnegie Hall in 1966 may stand:

> 'Richard Lewis' Captain Vere was a joy. Now that is a man who ought to be restrained in this city by force, to show every tenor around the way a musical line can be infused with style, warmth and pure, simple beauty.'
>
> *New York Herald Tribune*, 5.1.1966

In December, just one month after his death, the Royal Opera House, Covent Garden paid its tribute to Richard with a series of

Fidelio performances dedicated to his memory, conducted by Christoph von Dohnányi. Richard would have been delighted that this was a co-production involving the Théâtre Royal de la Monnaie, Brussels; in a way the city where his professional career began.

On 20th April 1991, a memorial concert was given in Ringmer Parish Church, and the Ditchling Choral Society under Janet Canetty-Clarke sang some of Richard's favourite music. The congregation included many of his old friends and colleagues who were there to lend their voices to the tributes paid him. A reception at Glyndebourne followed, where the great artist/designer Sir Hugh Casson sold six of Richard's paintings within an hour.

During the next three years Elizabeth looked for a way to provide a more permanent memorial to her husband, determined that this should be in the form of an award bearing his name, to enable one singer each year to train at the National Opera Studio. The Richard Lewis Award Fund Charitable Trust was established for this purpose, and her dreams were answered when, with the generosity of Dr Jean Shanks (Princess Yuri Galitzine), sufficient funds were provided to make this possible. With the collaboration of Glyndebourne, the wheels were set in motion for a valuable source of assistance within the profession.

Bearing in mind the many students of singing who could not benefit from the Jean Shanks-Richard Lewis Award, Elizabeth set about establishing a school in Eastbourne, where twice each year, short, intensive courses in opera, song, music theatre and the spoken word could be enjoyed by a relatively small group of students at various stages of development. Central to the training period would be a masterclass given by a distinguished artist working with the students in front of an audience and each course ending with a public concert. She was absolutely delighted when the Duke of Devonshire agreed to be the school's Patron.

The success of the Richard Lewis School of Performing Arts during three years has been such that early application to attend is now essential. Masterclasses have been given by Marjorie Thomas, John Carol Case, Derek Hammond-Stroud and Ian Partridge.

In March 1996, the BBC recorded a special programme devoted to Richard and presented by his old colleague Robert Tear.

During a very long career, Richard sang with virtually every great conductor in the world – Herbert von Karajan for some reason an exception. He was born to sing, and his collaboration with others similarly gifted gave him great joy. As early as 1950, Richard noted in his diary the names of some of the conductors he had worked with. It is an incredible list for such a short working life: Ansermet, André, Barbirolli, Beecham, van Beinum, Boult, Busch, Désormière, Enesco, Koussevitsky, Krips, Kubelik, Rankl, Raybould, de Sabata, Sargent, Schwartz, Süsskind, Tuxen and de Vocht. Before his career ended, the names of Bernstein, Klemperer, Ormandy, Previn, Walter *et al.* would be added.

As a young musician I knew Richard slightly. He was the great tenor, I a trumpeter in the orchestra. I could not have imagined that I would one day write his biography, and yet he was a figure who captured my imagination from the first and I observed him closely. He appeared to be touched with greatness even before he began to sing. It was not simply his confidence, though that was formidable: rather, it was an inspirational quality, drawn, I suspect, from another place.

Noel Ross-Russell, 1996

For further details about the Richard Lewis School of Performing Arts, contact:

Mrs Su Shanson
Administrator
The Richard Lewis School of Performing Arts
Pelham Cottage
120 Wish Hill
Willingdon
East Sussex
BN20 9HL

Tel: 01323 509035

Index

A

A Child of Our Time 103
Adler, Kurt Herbert 74, 76, 77, 118
Agon 75
Albert Hall (Manchester) 37, 51, 58, 65
Albert Herring 45, 47, 53, 60
Alceste 58, 66, 67, 79, 89
Alkmene 86
Allin, Norman 24, 34, 35, 36, 37
Alwyn, Kenneth 110
André, Franz 129
Andry, Peter 118
Ansermet, Ernest 129
Apollo Singers 4
Apostles, The 55
Aprahamian, Felix 70
Ardwick 3, 4, 41, 45
Ariadne auf Naxos 58, 65, 66, 67, 77, 81, 90
Arroyo, Martina 105
Ashkenazy, Vladimir 87
Auden, W.H. 61
Austin University 109

B

B Minor Mass 54
Bach, Johann Sebastian 42, 101, 103, 110
Bach Aria Group 83, 100, 101
Baden Street 3, 9, 28, 121
Baker, Dame Janet 56
Baker, Richard 83
Barbirolli, Lady, 52
Barbirolli, Sir John 52, 53, 56, 81, 95, 109, 114, 129
Barenboim, Daniel 87
Baron, Samual 83
Barrett, Herbert 77, 79, 81, 83, 84, 94, 114, 118
BBC Symphony Orchestra 18, 25, 29
Beecham, Sir Thomas 54, 81, 129
Beethoven, Ludwig van 29, 51, 58, 95, 105
Belsize Park Gardens 44
Benedictus 116
Berg, Alban 66, 100, 127
Bergonzi, Carlo 67

Berlin Opera 86
Berlioz, Hector 52, 58
Bernhard, Prince of the
  Netherlands 46
Bernstein, Leonard 125, 129
Billy Budd 95, 100, 127
Bing, Rudolf 41
Bishop, Irene 122, 123
Bizet, Georges 92
Bjoerling, Jussi 105
Bok, Mary Louise 104
Borg, Kim 56, 57
Borgioli, Dino 14, 27, 28
Boris Godunov 53, 75
Boult, Sir Adrian 84, 129
Bradbury, Fred 15
Brahms, Johannes 24
Brain, Dennis 46
Brannigan, Owen 48
Brearley, Dr Herman 24
Britten, Benjamin 39, 40, 41, 45,
  46, 47, 48, 58, 60, 64, 66, 91,
  95, 100, 103, 115, 116, 119
Bryn-Jones, Delmé 89
Brussels Conservatoire 39, 46
Brussels Philharmonic Orchestra
  39, 40
Brymer, Jack 59, 60
Busch, Fritz 129
Busoni, Ferruccio 84, 98

C

Caballé, Montserrat 105
Calico Printers Association
  (CPA) 6, 8, 9, 10, 14, 26, 27,
  29, 33, 34, 37, 41, 72, 80, 108
Callaway, Paul 107
Cameron, John 56
Canetty-Clark, Janet 115, 128
Cantata Academica 103
Canticum Sacrum 75

Caplat, Moran 53, 69, 93, 118
Carl Rosa Opera 37, 50
Carmen 73, 74, 92
Carol Case, John 128
Carr, Norman and Joan 118, 121,
  124
Casson, Sir Hugh 128
Central Hall (Manchester) 15, 19
Chandler, Kay 88, 89, 90, 93,
  117
Charles, Millie 10, 11, 26, 29,
  30, 33, 34, 38
Chicago Symphony Orchestra 84
Childhood of Christ, The 52
Chitty, Stella 100
Choral Symphony, The 58
Christie, Sir John 27, 81, 93, 94
Christie, George 81, 117
Christie, Mary 117
Coates, Edith 90
Colclough, Beryl 37, 113
Colclough, Richard 37, 38, 105,
  113
Coleridge-Taylor, Samuel 15
Collier, Marie 90
Concertgebouw 116
Constable, John 91
Corelli, Franco 67, 105
Coronation Mass 74
Così fan Tutte 48, 53, 58, 74, 75,
  83, 94
Cottle, Mary 39
Covent Garden 36, 48, 50, 51,
  53, 54, 55, 56, 58, 61, 66, 68,
  72, 73, 75, 88, 90, 91, 97, 99,
  100, 107, 113, 118, 124, 128
Cross, Joan 45, 51
Cuénod, Hugues 83, 116
Curtis Institute 104, 109

D

Darley, Sylvia 111
Das Lied von der Erde 58, 77, 84, 86, 95, 116
Davies, David Ffrangcon 28
Davies, Sir Walford 14
Davis, Andrew 114
Davis, Sir Colin 114
Dawber, Harold 24
de Falla, Manuel 113
de Sabata, Victor 129
de Vocht, Lodewijk 129
Deansgate Cinema 25
Désormière, Roger 129
Devonshire, Duke of 128
Didsbury Central High School 4, 6, 8, 9
Die Fledermaus 100
Die Zauberflöte– see also The Magic Flute 85, 86, 87, 124
Di Stefano, Giuseppe 67
Ditchling Choral Society 115, 128
Doktor Faustus 84, 98
Domingo, Placido 87
Don Giovanni 27, 54, 85, 91, 92, 100
Donizetti, Gaetano 42
Dowland, John 91
Dream of Gerontius, The – see *Gerontius*
Duparc, Henri 91

E

Ebert, Carl 61
Edward VIII, King 17
Edwards, David 28
Edwards, Gwyneth (later Gwyneth Mitchell) 28, 93, 107, 108, 123

Edwards, Vera (see also Vera Thomas) 28, 31, 71, 92, 93, 107, 108, 113, 113, 123
Electra 112, 115
Elgar, Sir Edward 25, 55, 56, 74, 96, 113
Elijah 82, 105
Elizabeth II, Queen 92
Elwes, Gervase 25, 57, 65
Enesco, Georges 129
ENSA 7
Essex Road 28, 31, 48, 77
Evans, Sir Geraint 64, 65, 66, 81, 87, 118, 124
Evans, Thomas 4, 5, , 7, 11, 14, 15, 16, 22, 23, 24

F

Fair Maid of Perth, The 92
Fairfield 79, 85
Fairy Queen 58
Ferrier, Kathleen 48, 74
Fidelio 88, 93, 107, 128
Fischer-Dieskau, Dietrich 84
Flagstaad, Kirsten 40
Forbes, R.J. 34
Ford, Harold 108
Ford, Vera 108
Forrester, Maureen 83, 105
Frankenstein, Alfred 74
Free Trade Hall (Manchester) 56
From Olivet to Calvary 32
Fuller, Frederick 121

G

Galitzine, Princess Yuri (Dr. Jean Shanks) 128
Gerontius 25, 52, 55, 56, 57, 58, 65, 74, 76, 77, 81, 95, 96, 107, 109, 110, 113, 114, 115, 116, 126

Gigli, Beniamino 18, 67
Gilbert and Sullivan 78, 83
Gilday, Edwin F. 113
Glyndebourne Opera 27, 41, 47, 53, 54, 58, 59, 60, 61, 66, 67, 69, 74, 75, 79, 80, 81, 82, 83, 85, 88, 90, 93, 94, 95, 102, 106, 107, 108, 110, 116, 117, 118, 123, 128
Goehr, Walter 46
Gondoliers, The 83
Granger, Stewart 64
Greenhouse, Bernard 83
Grieg, Edvard 40
Grier, Dr Arnold 65
Griffiths, Wyn 67

H

HaakonVII , HM King of Norway 40
Hall, Peter 97, 98, 99
Hallé Orchestra 6, 18, 24, 25, 30, 52, 55
Hammond-Stroud, Derek 128
Handel, George Frederick 15, 41, 43, 83, 90, 92, 95, 108, 110
Handel-Haydn Orchestra 113
Hassall, Christopher 63
Hasse, Adolf 42
Hawkins, Margaret
Hazel Grove 15
Heaton Moor Methodist Guild 17
Hester, Dr. Joan 124
Hiawatha 15
Hines, Jerome 62
Hope-Johnson, Philip 46
Hughes, Arwel 67
Hughes, David 89
Hutton, Leonard (Len) 26

I

Idomeneo 54, 58, 66
Il Ritorno d'Ulisse 106, 107, 116
Il Seraglio 34, 53, 60
Isaacs, Edward 31
Isepp, Martin 91, 101, 118
Ingpen, Joan 77

J

Janacek, Leos 94
Jenufa 92
Jephtha 91
Jones, Cai 34
Jones, Leslie 17
Juliana, Princess of the Netherlands 46

K

Kallman, Chester 62
Karajan, Herbert von 127
Karg, Baron 85
Kellock, Mary (see also Mary Lewis) 124
Kennedy, Michael 52
Kent, HRH Duke of 22, 23, 93
King, James 105
King Priam 89, 90, 105, 107, 112
Kirkby, Mary – see Mary Cottle
Klebe, Giselher 86
Klemperer, Otto 87, 124, 129
Knowles, Albert 34
Kochen, Pacho 42
Kodály, Zoltan 58
Koussevitzky, Serge 129
Krauss, Otakar 70, 90
Krips, Josef 74, 129
Kubelik, Rafael 18, 74, 118, 129

L

La Bohème 36, 92
La Clemenza di Tito 69
Lancaster, Osbert 61
Langdon, Michael 66
Langridge, Phillip 82-3, 127
Lanigan, John 68
La Scala, Milan 87
Laszlo, Magda 64, 90
La Traviata 58, 68
La Vida Breve 54
Lear, Evelyn 86
Legge, Walter 63, 64
Leigh, Adèle 68, 69, 70
Leinsdorf, Erich 105
Les Illuminations 39, 40, 76
Les Noces 46
Leppard, Raymond 106
Lewis, Elizabeth (née Robertson)
    79, 80, 81, 84, 85, 92, 93, 95,
    100, 101 103, 106, 107, 108,
    110, 111, 113, 114, 115, 116,
    117, 119, 120, 120, 121, 122,
    123, 124, 125, 128
Lewis, Huilee 124, 126
Lewis, Mary – aka Mary Thomas
    – (see also Mary Lingard and
    Mary Kellock) 41, 43, 50, 51,
    52, 54, 57, 71, 72, 75, 76, 77,
    84, 99, 105
Lewis, Michael 57, 71, 73, 75,
    76, 77, 80, 84, 92, 100, 101,
    102, 103, 105, 107, 115, 118,
    121, 123, 124, 125, 126
Lewis, Nigel 102, 103, 107, 108,
    111, 114, 115, 121, 123, 124,
    125
Lewis, Richard 40-129 *passim*
Lewis, Thomas Zhen 126
L'Incoronazione di Poppea 83,
    90, 95
Lingard, Joseph 30, 52

Lingard, Mary (see also Mary
    Lewis) 30, 34, 38
Littleton, Rt.Hon.Oliver 45
Llansantffraid 1, 3, 4
Lloyd, David 27, 62
London Road Station 15
Lord, Annie 24, 35
Lord's Prayer 120
Lorengar, Pilar 68
Lough, Ernest 15
Ludwig, Leopold 66
Lulu 100

M

MacAnn, Rodney 114
Madam Butterfly 73, 75
Magic Flute, The - see also *Die
    Zauberflöte* 55, 61, 74, 85
Mahler, Gustav 58, 116
Marshall, Lois 83
Maunder, John 32
Melik-Pashaev, Alexander 89
Mendelssohn, Felix 82
Menges, Herbert 45, 46
Menna 67
Merriman, Nan 62
Messiah 14, 16, 35, 45, 54, 55,
    58, 110, 112
Mewton-Wood, Noel 91
Midland Hotel 18, 19
Midsummer Marriage, The 52,
    54, 68, 69, 89
Mikado, The 83
Milnes, Sherrill 105
Milwaukee Symphony Orchestra
    113
Missa Solemnis 51, 105
Mitchell, Eric 108
Mitchell, Gwyneth – see
    Gwyneth Edwards
Monteverdi, Claudio 90, 106
Moore, Gerald 91

Morgan, Edward 90
Morison, Elsie 48, 62, 67
Moseley, Agnes 34
Moses and Aaron 97, 98, 99,100, 101, 105, 112
Mozart, Wolfgang Amadeus 17, 35, 41, 42, 48, 55, 60, 66, 70, 74, 75, 91, 110

N

Nansen Street 4
Napier, Diana 39
Nash, Heddle 25, 55, 56, 57, 92
National Symphony Orchestra 107
Newman, Cardinal 56, 57
Nicholson, Mary 81
Nielsen, Birgit 112
Nuits d'Eté 58

O

Offenbach, Jacques 95
On Wenlock Edge 36, 115
Ormandy, Eugene 82, 88, 104, 105, 129
Oslo Philharmonic Orchestra 40
Oxford Square 45, 46

P

Parsons, Geoffrey 90, 105, 118
Partridge, Ian 128
Paul, James 83, 113, 114, 127
Pavarotti, Luciano 69, 87, 118
Pears, Peter 45, 46, 47, 48, 64, 66, 83, 95
Pergolesi, Giovanni 42
Peter Grimes 48, 51, 53, 54, 60, 61, 64
Philadelphia Orchestra 82, 88, 104

Pinner 23, 50, 55, 57, 72, 79
Prague Philharmonic Orchestra 18
Preston-Roberts, Michael 109, 110
Previn, André 129
Proctor, Norma 48
Psalmus Hungaricus 58
Puccini, Giacomo 92

Q

Queen of Spades 89
Queen's Park Theatre 19
Quilico, Louis 90

R

Rake's Progress, The 58, 59, 61, 62, 63, 69, [74], 81, 86, 92
Rankl, Karl 45, 129
Rape of Lucretia, The 45, 47, 60, 119
Raybould, Clarence 129
Reizenstein, Franz 91
Requiem (Mozart) 70, 74
Requiem (Verdi) 58, 76, 100
Rescue, The 54
Resnick, Regina 105
Richard I 95
Rickmansworth 50, 85, 117
Ring, The 97
Ripley, Gladys 74
Robertson, Betty 93
Robertson, Elizabeth – see Elizabeth Lewis
Robertson, Fyfe 80, 93, 108, 121
Robertson, Grace 100, 107, 121, 123
Robertson, Hilda 18, 20, 80
Robinson, Forbes 97, 113, 118
Rolfe Johnson, Anthony 109, 116

Ronald, Sir Landon 17, 31
Rosbaud, Hans 97
Rosenthal, Harold 118
Rothnie, Sir Alan and Lady 105, 106, 118
Rothwell, Evelyn (Lady Barbirolli) 52
Royal Academy of Music 26, 36, 44, 109
Royal Albert Hall 58, 65
Royal College of Music 27, 36, 80
Royal Festival Hall 58, 84
Royal Liverpool Philharmonic Orchestra 48, 114
Royal Manchester College of Music 8, 24, 27, 34, 36, 44
Royal Northern College of Music 8
Royal Opera House – see Covent Garden
Royal Schools of Music 22
Rycroft Park 34

S

Sacrum Canticum 59
Sadler's Wells 36, 48, 53, 95, 108
Salomé 105
Santa Cecilia Orchestra 112
Sargent, Sir Malcolm 25, 51, 52, 56, 64, 65, 96, 109, 111, 113, 114, 126, 129
Scarlatti, Alessandro 42
Scheide, William 101
Schoenberg, Arnold 97, 98
Schwarz, Rudolf 129
Seasons, The 54
Serenade for Tenor, Horn and Strings 40, 45, 54, 66, 115
Serkin, Rudolf 104
Shirley, George 110

Shumsky, Oscar 83
Siepi, Cesare 105
Simoneau, Leopold 75, 104, 105, 118
Sinclair, Monica 64
Smith, Joy 126
Solti, Sir Georg 82, 88, 97, 98, 100, 118
Song of the Earth – see *Das Lied von der Erde*
Spring Symphony 58, 116
St. Andrews 117
St Ann's Church 38
St James' Palace 22
St. John Passion 54
St. Louis Symphony Orchestra 77
St. Matthew Passion 35, 55, 110, 113, 115
St Paul's School 38
Steinberg, William 113
Stewart, Thomas 86
Stiff, Wilfred 48, 51, 52, 79, 84, 118
Strauss, Richard 36, 66, 77, 81, 90
Stravinsky, Igor 46, 59, 62, 74, 75, 86, 92
Süsskind, Walter 129
Sutherland, Dame Joan 68, 69, 70

T

Tales of Hoffmann, The 95
Tauber, Richard 12, 14, 39, 40, 60
Tear, Robert 129
Tchaikovsky, Peter Ilyich 89
Te Deum 55
Théâtre Royal de la Monnaie, Brussels 53, 128

Thomas, Marjorie 36, 65, 81,
    105 113, 128
Thomas, Mary 1, 3, 4, 5, 7, 9, 11,
    13, 28, 31, 55, 71
Thomas, Thomas 1, 2, 9, 11, 13,
    28, 31, 41, 54, 55
Thomas, Tom (see also Richard
    Lewis) 1-43 *passim*, 108
Thomas, Vera (see also Vera
    Edwards) 1, 3, 4, 6
Thorndike, Dame Sybil 36
Three Cornered Hat, The 113
Thurston Hopkins, Godfrey 100,
    107, 121, 123
Timms, Ken 10, 14, 26, 33
Tippett, Sir Michael 69, 70, 89,
    98, 103
Tooley, Sir John 55, 56, 63, 68
    89, 90, 118
Tosca 25, 29, 34, 92
Toscanini, Arturo 18, 25, 29
Tourel, Jennie 86
Troilus and Cressida 63, 64, 65,
    66, 72, 73, 95
Turner, Dame Eva 65
Tuxen, Erik 129

U

Unrath, Jim 114

V

van Beinum, Eduard 129
Vaughan Williams, Ralph 36
von Dohnányi, Christoph 128

W

Wagner, Richard 97
Walker, Norman 48
Walker, Sarah 114
Wallenstein, Alfred 62, 73, 76

Wallenstein, Virginia 73, 76
Walter, Bruno 129
Walters, Jess 68
Walton, Sir William 63, 64, 65,
    66, 98
War Requiem 116
Webb, Brenda 118, 121, 122
Webster, Sir David 45, 48, 55,
    68, 99
Weingartner, Felix 25
Werber, Erik 85
Werther 89
Williams, John 90
Wozzeck 66, 92, 115
Wood, Lorna 17
Wright Greaves 17, 19

Y

Yeomen of the Guard, The 78

Z

Zareska, Eugenia 116
Zimbalist, Efrem 104

Discography

This discography lists those recordings of Richard Lewis which are available at the time of publication.

EMI/Testament recordings

Beethoven: *Mass in C Minor*; CDM 7 64385 2; with Jennifer Vyvyan, Monica Sinclair, Marian Nowakowski, Beecham Choral Society, Royal Philharmonic Orchestra, Sir Thomas Beecham.

Elgar: *Dream of Gerontius*; CMS 7 63185 2 (2 CDs) (Gerontius); with Dame Janet Baker, Kim Borg, Hallé Choir, Sheffield Philharmonic Chorus, Ambrosian Singers, Hallé Orchestra, Sir John Barbirolli.

Mendelssohn: *Elijah*; CDCFPSD 4802 (2 CDs); with Elsie Morison, Marjorie Thomas, John Cameron, Huddersfield Choral Society, Royal Philharmonic Orchestra, Sir Malcolm Sargent.

Mozart: *Così fan Tutte* (excerpts); SBT 1040; (Ferrando); with Sena Jurinac, Blanche Thebom, Erich Kunz, Mario Borriello, Glyndebourne Festival Orchestra, Fritz Busch.

Sullivan: *The Gondoliers*; CMS 7 64394 2 (2 CDs); (Marco Palmieri); with Geraint Evans, Monica Sinclair, Elsie Morison, John Cameron, Marjorie Thomas, Alexander Young, Owen Brannigan, Helen Watts, Glyndebourne Festival Chorus, Pro Arte Orchestra, Sir Malcolm Sargent.

Sullivan: *The Mikado*; CMS 7 64403 2 (2 CDs); (Nanki-Poo); with Owen Brannigan, Geraint Evans, Elsie Morison, Ian Wallace, Marjorie Thomas, Monica Sinclair, John Cameron, Jeannette Sinclair, Glyndebourne Festival Chorus, Pro Arte Orchestra, Sir Malcolm Sargent.

Sullivan: *H.M.S. Pinafore*; CMS 7 64397 2 (2 CDs); with (Ralph Rackstraw); George Baker, John Cameron, Elsie Morison, Owen Brannigan, James Milligan, Marjorie Thomas, Monica Sinclair, Glyndebourne Festival Chorus, Pro Arte Orchestra, Sir Malcolm Sargent.

Sullivan: *Pirates of Penzance*; CMS 7 64409 2 (2 CDs) (Frederic); with George Baker, James Milligan, Elsie Morison, Owen Brannigan, John Cameron, Monica Sinclair, Marjorie Thomas, Harold Blackburn, Glyndebourne Festival Chorus, Pro Arte Orchestra, Sir Malcolm Sargent.

Sullivan: *Ruddigore*; CMS 7 64412 2 (2 CDs) (Richard Dauntless); George Baker, Elsie Morison, Monica Sinclair, Elizabeth Harwood, Pamela Bowden, Owen Brannigan, Joseph Rouleau, Harold Blackburn, Glyndebourne Festival Chorus, Pro Arte Orchestra, Sir Malcolm Sargent.

Sullivan: *Trial by Jury*; CMS 7 64397 2 (2 CDs); (Defendant); with George Baker, Elsie Morison, John Cameron, Owen Brannigan, Bernard Turgeon, Glyndebourne Festival Chorus, Pro Arte Orchestra, Sir Malcolm Sargent.

Sullivan: *Yeomen of the Guard*; CMS 7 64415 2 (Colonel Fairfax); with Geraint Evans, Elsie Morison, John Carol Case, Alexander Young, Marjorie Thomas, Monica Sinclair, Denis Dowling, Owen Brannigan, Glyndebourne Festival Chorus, Pro Arte Orchestra, Sir Malcolm Sargent.

Walton: *Troilus and Cressida* (excerpts); CDM 64199 2 (Troilus); with Elisabeth Schwarzkopf, Monica Sinclair, Lewis Thomas, Geoffrey Walls, John Hauxvell, Philharmonia Orchestra, William Walton.

BMG Classics Recordings

Mahler: *Das Lied von der Erde*; 60178 2 RG, RCA Victor Gold Seal; with Maureen Forrester; Chicago Symphony Orchestra, Fritz Reiner.

Strauss: *Salomé*; 6644 2 RG, RCA Victor Gold Seal; with Montserrat Caballé, Sherrill Milnes, Regina Resnick, James King soloists, London Symphony Orchestra, Erich Leinsdorf.